# COLLEGE
# KNOWLEDGE
# for the Student Athlete

DAVID SCHOEM AND SHELLY KOVACS
The University of Michigan

Ann Arbor
THE UNIVERSITY OF MICHIGAN PRESS

ISBN-13: 978-0-472-03454-3

2014   2013   2012   2011          4   3   2   1

*For Our Students*

# INTRODUCTION

We have written this book to support the academic success of each and every college student athlete. We want them to succeed academically and athletically in college and to graduate so they can realize their life's hopes and dreams.

College athletics is very popular in the United States. As the authors of this book, our love of college athletics goes beyond the thrill of athletic accomplishments to the personal well-being and academic success of each and every college student athlete. While all college students must learn to negotiate the complicated transition from high school to college, there are unique and layered challenges for student athletes.

At the time this book went to press, athletic programs at a number of major universities were facing highly publicized scandals for alleged rules violations involving student athletes, coaches, boosters, and businesses. College athletic programs are under enormous pressure to demonstrate academic success by their student athletes. In order to maintain eligibility, schools and athletes are required to comply 100 percent with very specific and technical NCAA regulations that govern progress toward degree completion and academic achievement on a term-by-term and yearly basis. This is a high-stakes enterprise. We believe the current environment makes it even more urgent that student athletes, their parents, coaches, and advisors read this book carefully and completely. The consequences of not understanding the tips in *College Knowledge for the Student Athlete* could prevent student athletes from realizing their academic and athletic dreams.

We hope this book will serve as a road map and tour guide for a successful college experience and education. Each of the tips and vignettes is based on our own scholarship and experience as well as the wisdom and advice of our current and former students. The tips are also grounded in an extensive and substantive body of research about success in college. While many of the suggestions are relevant for all college students, they are directed specifically to the kinds of situations that are particular to the student athlete. We encourage student athletes to read the book from beginning to end the first time through. However, our experience has been that the most useful guidebook is one that readers can return to repeatedly, and we urge student athletes to keep this book in easy reach so that they can refer to it when facing new or unexpected challenges and opportunities during college.

We have written this book primarily for student athletes at large colleges and universities, but we believe that student athletes in other types of institutions will find most of the tips and vignettes applicable to their experiences as college athletes as well. While the characteristics, culture, and sport of each school will obviously affect the overall experience of each student athlete, the tips and vignettes in this book will resonate with any student who identifies himself or herself as an athlete and shares that common experience. This book will also serve as an excellent resource for parents, coaches, and mentors of student athletes.

There is wide diversity of experience among student athletes at the same school, regardless of the size of their college or university. Some student athletes compete as a member of a team while others participate in individual competitions. Some sports have dozens on their team while other sports have a smaller group. Some sports have historically attracted students of different racial, ethnic, and class backgrounds so that the demographic composition in any given sport may vary widely. There are often differences in the culture and dynamics of a women's team as opposed to a men's team. Some student athletes play in the limelight of national public attention and their sports attract large crowds while others may play before a crowd comprised mostly of devoted family and friends. There are scholarship athletes and non-scholarship athletes whose experiences differ based on their financial situation. Different sports compete at different times of the year, and some athletes compete in more than one sport. There are differences, too, for those athletes who compete in sports typically considered revenue-generating, like football, basketball, ice hockey, and baseball, and those who compete in sports like golf, tennis, wrestling, or lacrosse.

In writing this book, we have attempted to address the tips to fit as many student athletes as possible in this rich array of diverse experiences, but readers will find that a specific sentence, paragraph, tip, or vignette may apply more to one set of athletes than to another. We urge readers to continue reading to learn more about the experiences of other student athletes and to identify the commonalities across the experience of all student athletes.

For more than 30 years, we have been fortunate to have college students share their academic and personal successes, challenges, and life stories with us. We have been first-hand observers of what has helped them learn, grow, excel, and graduate. We have also heard and seen which approaches to college have not worked so well. We hope all of our students have learned from their time with us, and we are heartened by the many students who remain in touch with us long after their college experience. Just as they have learned from us, we now want to thank all of our students for all that we have learned from them. In writing this book, we pass along their wisdom to future generations of student athletes.

Shelly Kovacs has worked with college students for more than three decades. She is the Director of Student Services at the University of Michigan School of Kinesiology and has worked with student athletes throughout her career in higher education. She is well known and highly regarded for her commitment to providing the best possible educational experience for her students.

Shelly has received particular recognition for her success working with student athletes, including graduating athletes who left college before finishing their degrees. She has been instrumental in the development and implementation of several cutting-edge initiatives for student athletes at Michigan, including an academic support program for student athletes with learning disabilities and the evolution of an academic support staff using collaborative models of academic advising.

Shelly's work with athletes has been an outgrowth of the first model of academic skills assessment for student athletes at the University of Michigan, which she developed in 1976. While she has served on many task forces and committees addressing issues that have shaped the infrastructure of the student athlete experience at Michigan, Shelly takes greatest pride in her ability to change the lives of her students, one by one and day by day. She has presented workshops and seminars to audiences at the national, state, and university levels covering a wide range of higher educational issues and has served on the boards of national and state organizations in academic affairs administration. As the recipient of various awards and honors over the years, Shelly's most coveted awards are the endowed scholarship established in her honor in 2010 by former students and the Honorary M Letter she received in 2003 from the Michigan Varsity Letter Winner's Club in recognition of her service and commitment to athletes at the University of Michigan. At that time, she was one of only a handful of women to receive this prestigious award.

David Schoem is a first-generation college student, holding degrees from the University of Michigan, Harvard University, and the University of California at Berkeley. As a graduate of Overbrook High School (a large, public, urban high school in Philadelphia known for its championship teams and future NBA stars), David is deeply committed to the promise of public education and an educated public, to educational equity, and to giving back to all of those promising and capable individuals, like the many he attended school with, who either didn't graduate high school or who never continued their studies beyond high school. (David's one regret is not having made the basketball team at Overbrook High despite his great success playing street ball in the alley behind his house.)

David is the Director of the Michigan Community Scholars Program at the University of Michigan and has spent his entire career there enough. My parents, probably unknowingly, provided the support and inspiration in the early years of my career that led me down this path. My father's pride and my mother's joy in my accomplishments remain with me and were very much part of the genesis of this book.

David Schoem: I wish to thank my loving family for this, my tenth book. My wife, Karyn, and adult daughters, Adina and Shana, have offered constant encouragement. Karyn has been patient beyond words during this past intensive year of book writing. My father, Gerald, was passionately devoted to higher education, despite his never having received a college degree and, my mother, Sara, now 88 years old, has always represented the most vocal and heartfelt cheering section for my every endeavor.

# CONTENTS

# The Top 10 Tips for a Championship Education

## 1. Believe in Both of You: The College Student and the College Athlete

The importance of maintaining your self-confidence in college cannot be overstated. If you practice good study habits and have the desire to succeed, you will do just that at each and every college that offered you admission. Know that this is true, remind yourself daily, and never question your intellectual abilities.

There is a mind game that gets played out at every college. Very simply, students worry that they're not up to the college's standard. Unfortunately, colleges do very little to allay such fears. First-year students look at their peers in the residence hall cafeteria, at the college convocation, at the first lecture or the first team meeting and worry that they're just not as smart as the other students. The reality, however, is that how well you do in college is not just about how smart you are. Instead, the key is developing good study skills, discovering your interests, meeting good students and faculty, and finding your own identity.

Most student athletes come to college with a strong belief in their athletic competence. In fact, it is part of your competitive spirit to believe that you landed on a college athletic team because you belong there. You may have been recruited by a few, even many, schools on the basis of your athletic prowess. But just like most new college students, most student athletes do not have that same level of confidence in their academic abilities when starting college. This dichotomy of feeling so confident in the athletic arena yet lacking confidence in yourself in the academic arena can sometimes create a self-fulfilling prophecy that can land you in academic trouble. You want to be successful in *both* athletics and academics. See also Tip 7 on pages 45–47.

One of the most valuable lessons you can acquire as a successful college student athlete is about transferable skills: how to transfer the athletic skills you already possess and have trained toward perfecting to the academic area of your life. You have trained to be focused and prepared, to have confidence in yourself, and to believe that practice makes perfect. These same principles apply to academic success.

Effort also plays a critical role in athletic and academic success. Any seasoned athlete knows a coach would choose the athlete with less natural ability and a strong work ethic over the athlete with more natural ability and a poor work ethic. Just as there will be athletes better than you and not as good as you, there will be students smarter than you and less smart than you. Your success will be determined, in large part, by what you do to attain the results you want.

Even the brightest students at the best schools experience feelings of academic inadequacy. You have the advantage of being trained to believe in yourself as part of your athletic development. Pay attention to the feedback you get from instructors as a helpful indicator of how you are *actually* performing, as opposed to how you think you're performing. Be as prepared for an exam as you would be for a game or meet. Don't be embarrassed to ask questions or ask for help. Believe in your right to be a student, believe in your ability to be successful, and allow your competitiveness to flow into your academic life. Above all else, believe in both parts of you, the student and the athlete.

## 2. Learn to Be a College Student

Chances are you visited your college while you were being recruited; so that when you arrived on campus to start college, you already had some familiarity with it. However, once you start going to class, you will appreciate that you did not fully understand what college would be like. College is an entirely different universe than high school, both athletically and academically. The easiest way to describe the difference is that college is more of everything—more expectations and demands both athletically and academically and more independence in how you live each day. Simply said, college is not Grade 13. This is true both academically and athletically.

Don't waste your time in college by approaching it as you approached high school. What worked for you in high school will not work for you in college, and, really, you wouldn't want it to. Athletically, everything will be more intense—preparation, practice, and competition. As a student athlete, you will be governed by the NCAA and conference rules. The compliance office in your athletic department will be your primary resource for following these rules. Don't take chances with your eligibility. The stakes are much greater than they were in high school.

Come to college mentally prepared and with the right expectations for your college learning experience. It's your time to be an independent adult thinker. You can assert your own ideas, interpretations, and analyses. You can, and should, get involved in the issues of the world. Be prepared to defend your ideas, opinions, values, decisions, and actions. This can be difficult, especially in your first year. But embrace this opportunity. Don't shy away from it.

Think about what skills you want to improve to help you do better in college. Then find out where you can learn those skills. Most students have not had formal instruction in note taking, study skills, time management, or test taking, yet these are fundamental skills that will make a difference in your college success. See also Tip 2 on pages 30–32, Tip 8 on pages 47–49, and Tip 2 on pages 56–57. Most college athletic programs provide academic and tutorial support that includes the opportunity to work on these skills.

Whether or not you know what you want to pursue in college, do not think you need to take all of your requirements right away. Balance your schedule with courses that count toward your requirements and courses you find interesting and exciting. See Tip 9 on pages 71–73.

Most new college students have not thought about taking courses in subjects not offered in their high schools. What steps can you take in your first year to help you transition from high school and to embrace the best that your college has to offer?

1. Take a small class or seminar in a subject that interests you. In a small class you will be with a faculty member who loves to get to know students, and you will get to explore the subject very differently than you would in a large class.
2. Take courses with good teachers. See also Tip 8 on pages 69–71. Regardless of how interested you are in any given course content or course description, you are better off selecting your courses on the basis of the best teachers you can find. Speak to your advisors and other students for suggestions (see also Tip 5 on pages 91–93).
3. Try out a new idea. It is the very essence of college.
4. Try out a course in a subject you've never considered before. See Tip 4 on pages 109–11.
5. Imagine a new career. See Tip 6 on pages 177–79.
6. Make new friends with students from all backgrounds (see also Tip 3 on pages 121–23).

## 3. Expand Your Comfort Zone

The first days of college can be intimidating socially as well as academically. After four or more years with the same group of friends, having established a reputation among your peers and teachers, having been a leader in school and community groups, and having been recognized as both an accomplished athlete and a special person, you now have to start all over. Or so it seems at the time. At this anxious moment, many students are inclined to withdraw to what feels most comfortable, which is their teammates and their high school circle of friends.

Teammates and high school friends are important, but it's a mistake to retreat to them just for security. It's a mistake because you don't want to repeat your high school experience.

College truly is the time for you to meet the world from which you've been protected for most of your life. See also Tips 2 and 3 on pages 119–23. As an athlete, your high school experience may have been broadened through travel to compete with students from outside your own school. Yet, most students entering college have not yet been exposed to many different types of people or experiences. And some college students come from neighborhoods and schools that are segregated by race, religion, and class. If you retreat to the comfort zone of your high school days, it's as if you are locking yourself in your room and imposing a strict curfew.

In college you have the opportunity to meet a whole range of new people with different backgrounds and different ideas from yours. They may see the world through very different lenses. Try on their lenses in addition to your own. It will sharpen your vision and will encourage others to want to learn more about you, as an individual, as a student, and as an athlete.

Look around your classrooms and you will see interesting and smart people. Look at the faces in your cafeteria. There you will find hundreds of talented people. Get to know some of these people. Each one has an inspiring life story that you should hear.

If you come from a big city, you will have the opportunity to meet people from small rural towns. In what ways do they view politics and interpret books different from or similar to you? If you come from a liberal background, talk to a conservative student and find out that person's perspective. If you are a student who could not afford to attend college without your athletic scholarship, get to know someone whose family can afford to fly that student home on weekends. What do you have in common, and in what ways are your worlds so different that it takes a special effort to speak a common language?

Students who embrace the diversity of their colleges are better prepared for participating in a diverse workforce, negotiating contracts with people from different backgrounds, and supervising or being supervised by a wide range of people.

## 4. Work Smarter, Not Harder, for Academic and Athletic Success

It may come as a surprise that for many students college success is as much a result of good study skills as it is of intellectual ability or "smarts." That's right. One of the most important elements of academic success in college is having good study skills. Your college already has made the determination that you are intellectually qualified to do good academic work. But translating your intellectual abilities into passing grades requires expertise in the how-to of studying. This is true for all college students, but especially for student athletes who essentially have two full-time jobs: school and sports.

There's no single best answer for everyone regarding study skills, but there certainly is a best approach for you as an individual. Where and under what conditions do you study best? Some students can concentrate quite well in their residence hall rooms with music playing, interruptions from neighbors, and a generally loud setting. Other students need to leave their living space and go to a library or an empty classroom to find the quiet and solitude necessary to concentrate, study, and write.

Most athletic departments require first-year student athletes and others to participate in what is called study table. This usually means going to a designated place to study for a minimum amount of time each day. Study hours can be during the day or evening hours, and tutors are usually available onsite or by scheduling tutor sessions. Be assertive about getting the help you need as soon as possible.

When you sit down to study, the first thing to do is get yourself organized. Review your assignments. What is due the next day, the next week, the next month? How long is each assignment likely to take? Which assignment are you mentally and physically prepared to focus on first? The most difficult assignment should have your deepest concentration. Know whether your study style is to immerse yourself in a single project for hours at a time or to work in 20- or 30-minute chunks. Pace yourself. Plan breaks.

In math and science, you will likely have problem sets to complete daily and weekly. It's important to keep up with these daily assignments but not at the expense of putting off longer term assignments. Do not even think about leaving long essays or research papers until a few days or even the night before the due date. Writing papers requires a process of thinking, rethinking, drafting, revising, rethinking again, redrafting again, and so on. Every paper you turn in should represent, at the very least, your third draft. And, reaching the third draft should represent a process of thinking, composing, and rethinking the content, language, style, and the technical aspects of the paper.

As you are about to begin on a specific assignment, go back and carefully reread the assignment. Make sure you understand it. Not only is it frustrating to work for hours on something only to realize that you didn't precisely address the written assignment, but your grade will reflect that mistake as well. In college you will only get points for outcome, not for effort. Be certain you understand what is expected, and don't hesitate to contact the instructor—but not at the last minute—for clarification if you have any questions.

Many students are not prepared for all the reading required in college courses. It is essential that you learn to read the wide range of text assignments in different ways. Reading history or chemistry textbooks requires a different approach than reading more popular non-fiction or fiction books. Scholarly journal articles and longer academic books require yet another level of focus and concentration to fully comprehend the research findings, empirical analysis, and theoretical discussion they reflect. Most students did not learn how to do this in high school, so make sure to learn how to do this type of reading when you get to college.

Don't sell yourself short in the area of study habits. Do a good, honest assessment of your study habits, and make adjustments and improvements as needed. Don't hesitate to ask for advice and suggestions to improve your study skills very early in your college career.

## 5. Ask for Help: That's Why You Need a Professor, a Coach, an Advisor, and a Compliance Officer

In high school, asking for academic help is often what distinguishes the students who are in academic difficulty or considered at risk from the "smart" students. In college, the whole notion of asking for academic help is entirely different from high school. Asking about a topic or to get a more detailed explanation reflects that you are engaged in the very process. Being able to ask for help is crucial, and the first step is acknowledging that you need help. However, there are rules for asking for help in college. You are expected to do your part first.

Instructors, advisors, or tutors will not take kindly to giving you individualized assistance if you did not attempt to do the required reading or homework. And it will be obvious to them. There is a huge leap between high school and college in the amount of work required and study time expected for most classes. Depending on the specific class and college, the norm for college work ranges from 2.0–3.0 clock hours of study time for each instructional or contact hour. That means if you are taking 12 credit hours, you should plan on 24–36 clock hours of study time. If that sounds too high to you, compare it to the number of hours you practice and prepare for your sport. Your grade is often a direct result of the amount of study time you put in outside of class. Short cuts that worked in high school will not work in college. Do not look to your instructors or tutors to bail you out of work that you did not take the time to do. But when you are doing your part, those in a position to assist you will most often be glad to help.

Universities are comprised of people genuinely interested in discovering, studying, learning, analyzing, creating, and sharing new knowledge. It is within that context that everyone in college, faculty and students alike, are in constant search of deeper, clearer understandings and new insights. If you don't understand the complexities of an argument, if you miss the meaning of a lecture, or if the math assignment or readings are not clear, then ask! See also Tip 6 on pages 43–45.

Your first stop for academic planning should be with an academic advisor, and it should be a frequent stop throughout your college years. See also Tip 3 on pages 32–35. Advisors know the academic rules and graduation requirements. They also have extensive experience guiding students through their college careers. They will try to help you make decisions about your college plans rather than outline plans for you. After all, this is *your* college education, not theirs, not your parents', not your teachers', not your coaches', and not your friends'.

As an athlete, you will have an advisor in your academic unit and most likely another advisor in your athletic department. Your academic unit advisor is your primary advisor who will assist you with everything related to your college student experience. Advisors in most athletic departments are responsible for academic support and ensuring that you remain eligible in accordance with the NCAA and conference rules about degree progress. Both types of advisors are concerned about your academic choices and decisions, but each views them through different lenses. The need to evaluate their perspectives is just one of many reasons why it's important to actively participate in your education.

Just as there are coaches and a number of other professionals who work with your athletic team to prepare you for competition, you also have a team of people to support your educational efforts. See Tip 3 on pages 32–35. Be sure to visit your course instructor. He or she will be best able to answer your specific course questions, help you understand a lecture or reading, teach you how to interpret an assignment, or explain what will be covered on the exam. In addition to your instructor, your academic team may also include a graduate student instructor (or teaching assistant), your academic advisor, an advisor in the athletic department, and tutors provided by the athletic department and/or other offices on campus.

Most colleges have a variety of learning labs and resource centers in which students can drop in or schedule appointments with specialists. See Tip 3 on pages 57–59. In math labs, students can do their math homework online, use computer programs, work in study groups, or utilize one-to-one tutorial help. Science resource centers offer computer software designed for specific classes to solve problems, complete homework, and study for exams. In traditional language labs, there may be a variety of computer programs, software, videos, and tutors. Writing centers help students conceptualize and organize papers, give feedback on drafts of paper assignments, and assist with mechanical skills such as grammar and composition. College libraries are much more comprehensive and technologically advanced than most high school libraries, and college librarians are eager to offer personal assistance to students to access computer databases and find sources in print and online for research papers.

Remember, if you're not asking for help and taking advantage of academic support services, including advisors, professors, study groups, and tutors, you're not working smart. Most of your learning will take place outside of the classroom, and you must be skilled and assertive to be sure your academic learning outside of class is as intensive, effective, and efficient as it is inside the classroom.

**Ricky Gray: "I want to be the best both in the classroom and on the football field."**

*In high school, Ricky was the best. Indeed, it seemed like Ricky was an All-American in everything—captain of the football team, 4.0 student, king of the homecoming parade, most likely to succeed, and Mr. Popularity. Ricky was the hometown rock star and American Idol all wrapped up in one.*

*Unlike most student athletes, Ricky didn't face the persistent financial fear of losing his athletic scholarship because his family had the means to support his college education with or without the financial support. As a result, he didn't have quite the same "live or die football" attitude as many of his teammates. Some of them were a little put off by his not having to worry about money and faulted him for what they perceived as his arrogant attitude. But Ricky had a big enough personality to win over most of his teammates and a strong enough work ethic on the field that he found he could actually get along with pretty much anyone.*

A few weeks into the semester, Ricky knew he wasn't doing as well in his classes as he should. The football practices leading up to the start of the season had been far more intense than anything he had experienced in high school. He had been completely consumed with football for the first six weeks. In truth, he felt that he had lost his balance and was absorbed by the "live or die football" mentality he had previously been able to put aside. He hadn't had time to think about classes or gain a clear understanding of the academic expectations of college.

Ricky started to skip a class here and there, and he found he was so tired from practice, watching films, going to the weight room, and everything related to football that he knew his academic work wasn't really top quality. In high school, Ricky had been able to focus more on football and less on academics during the season because he was smart enough to coast through his classes until the winter semester. Unfortunately, his high school strategy wasn't working at college.

One day, after he had nodded off during class, his professor told Ricky to come see him during office hours. The professor told Ricky that he could tell from an earlier paper and his class participation that he was clearly capable of doing A work in this class, but that he wasn't realizing his academic potential with his missed classes, drowsiness, and indifference to assignments. Ricky, always respectful, thanked the professor, and told him that with all his practices, he was having trouble getting enough sleep and keeping up, but he would try to do better.

"That's not good enough, Ricky," said his professor. "I know that on the football field you don't dare cross your coaches. You do what they say, or else. Well, that's the same rule I have in my class. I'm your coach in this class, and I expect you to do your very best work here. And, if you think it would help, I'd be happy to call the football coaches to work something out." The idea that his professor might call his coaches put the ultimate fear in Ricky, and he quickly said he'd get on track and that it wasn't necessary to make any calls.

Ricky's frustration increased because he knew there was a bigger problem. He wasn't living up to his academic goals and potential, but he also was not performing on the football field as well as he had expected. Ricky was lucky to have made a good friend in one of his classes. Like him, she was driven and had set high academic expectations for herself. She had sympathy for Ricky's situation but had little patience for his self-pity. She knew he could do much better and wouldn't let him off the hook for his mediocre performance. She encouraged him to get on track and "coached" him to study more effectively by following her lead in prioritizing his work differently and using better time management skills.

Ricky realized that academic success required the same kind of preparation and commitment as his athletic success. He starting following all the steps he had been told would make him a better student, including using a planner, meeting with his instructors, participating in class, not allowing himself to get behind, and asking for tutors when he needed them. He began to see similarities between football and school that he had not seen before; he became focused on learning to play and study smarter, not just harder. At football practice, he paid closer attention to his strength and conditioning regimen, he listened to his coaches' instruction instead of assuming that his innate talent alone would be enough for success, and he actively worked to build better rapport with his teammates. Occasionally, he would be *tempted to lapse back into his high school patterns, but he knew that what worked in high school just didn't work in college. Ricky was no longer the football star he had been in high school, but he was on the verge of making a breakthrough in both football and academics that would lead to his success in life.*

## 6. Stay Eligible: Compliance and the NCAA

It is essential that you pay close attention to everything your compliance officers and athletic advisors tell you about eligibility rules. Maintaining your eligibility as a student athlete should always be on your mind. While you can't anticipate every situation you may find yourself in, you do need to know that a wide set of strict rules exist that govern and even sometimes intrude into your personal life. Most important, do not ever assume anything in relation to compliance or eligibility. You need to know what situations to avoid and to train yourself to frequently raise questions and get answers from the compliance staff. It is in the best interest of you and your school to make sure you have all the information you need to not risk your eligibility.

There are references throughout this book about the importance of abiding by the rules and regulations of the NCAA (www.ncaa.org/wps/wcm/connect/public/ncaa/resources) (and/or other smaller college athletic associations) and those of your conference, school, and athletic department (see Tip 1, pages 27–29; Tip 3, pages 32–35; Tip 5, pages 37–39; Tip 9, pages 49–51; Tip 8, pages 69–71; Tip 11, pages 76–78; Tip 1, pages 79–82; Tip 3, 83–86; Tip 8, pages 97–99; Tip 5, pages 147–49; Tip 9, page 158–62; and Tip 3, pages 168–71).

The complexity, specificity, and ever-changing nature of these rules can be overwhelming, even to professional compliance staff and advisors. In fact, the NCAA even governs your school's accountability and responsibility in communicating these rules to you. You will be given information on a regular basis, starting with your official and unofficial recruiting visits, so pay attention. Even if you are a walk-on, these rules affect your status.

College athletics in its organizational structure is a huge, complex business and becomes much more complicated every year. The intent of the many rules and regulations is to protect student athletes and to ensure that schools do not exploit their athletes at the expense of their degrees. Whether or not you agree with each and every rule is beside the point. As a student athlete, you are required to be in compliance *with each and every rule.* Too often—and at great personal and institutional expense as well as harsh national and international publicity—student athletes, coaches, and colleges are found to be in violation of NCAA rules. You never, ever, want to part of that kind of situation. Always make sure you are in compliance.

Every student athlete needs to pay particular attention to issues of gifts, money, academic probation, agents and secondary agents, prescription drugs and other illegal substances, etc. Student athletes are subject to rules and regulations that are more vast and often don't pertain to other college students. In order to remain eligible, you (and your family) must develop a working knowledge of these rules that govern your actions and behavior, as well as the actions and behaviors of others, such as boosters, but also friends and family. At times, it may appear that these rules dictate personal and family issues that have little to do with your status as a college student. Keep in mind that the rules exist because of previously identified problems in the past with those same issues.

There are two keys to keeping your athletic eligibility and scholarship intact: (1) follow each and every rule every day with no exceptions and (2) develop a red flag mentality about every action, behavior, or communication that could be problematic. The first one is tangible but requires knowing the rules. The second is more difficult because it is abstract. As a college athlete, you need to be sensitized to the types of actions and interactions that could raise concern, and your automatic response should be to contact your compliance office. Given the media attention to college athletics, especially when high-profile teams or players are sanctioned by the NCAA and/or their conference, you have surely been made aware of the consequences of not following the rules. To prevent these kinds of situations, compliance officers will provide you with information about what you can and cannot do. It is always up to you to follow the rules and, to the extent that you can influence fellow athletes, help ensure that other athletes follow the rules, too. Penalties for violating the rules are levied on teams and schools, not just individuals.

Know, too, that the rules to ensure you earn your degree as a college athlete can impact your academic and curricular choices. Your academic unit advisor may not be aware of the rules that impact your eligibility. You should both consult with your athletic department advisor regarding eligibility rules and also learn to be your own advocate. Know how many credits you must pass each term and each year. Know what happens if you take too many credits that are not applicable toward your degree and what degree applicability means. What happens if you get a C- in a required course or if the major you want requires a certain course or separate application? What happens if you take an independent study class, an online class, or a class at another school? These are examples of regulations that will affect you differently than they will affect your non-athlete counterparts. It can sometimes be more difficult or risky for athletes to change majors or explore challenging courses. Ironically, in the interest of ensuring that college athletes are able to earn their degrees, one unintended consequence of the rules is that student athletes sometimes do not have the same latitude or freedom to change majors as other students.

Athletic compliance can be compromised by anybody in any number of ways, so it should be viewed as the responsibility of everyone (students, parents, fans, coaches, etc.) to keep the university compliant and the athletes eligible.

## 7. Take Care of Yourself and Stay Out of Trouble

Balance is a core principle for having a successful college experience. It is essential to take care of your mind *and* body while you're in college. The stress and intensity are very real.

It is imperative that you eat well and make time to get enough sleep. See Tip 2 on pages 139–41. As important as this is for all college students, it is even more important for athletes. While you are training and competing, you are expending a great deal of mental and physical energy. You need to fuel your mind and your body to be successful.

It's also important to remember to laugh, smile, and have fun. Try to get away from campus every now and then, even if it's just for an hour or two. Go to the nearest downtown, watch a movie off campus, or work on a community service project that takes you off campus. If it's possible, go home even for a short visit. Treat yourself with respect. You deserve it. And, by the way, treat your peers with the very same level of respect.

Make good choices about your lifestyle if you want to stay competitive in your classes and in your sport. Remember if you use drugs or alcohol you are violating the rules of your college, your athletic conference, the NCAA (or other similar associations), and you are likely breaking the law. You could very easily jeopardize everything you've worked so hard for until now. Don't blow it. See Tip 5 on pages 147–49.

Don't let trouble find you either. Most assaults, fights, and other problems happen after midnight. Be mindful of whom you're hanging out with and watch the clock. Go home early and safely. See Tip 6 on pages 149–52.

Do not allow anyone to be verbally or physical violent or abusive toward you and do not permit any violence in your environment. All college campuses have mechanisms to report violence and provide counseling services as needed. If you are not sure about the boundaries for acceptable behavior or don't know whom to call or how to find out whom to call, start out with the campus operator or home page of the college website.

Take care of yourself physically. Enjoy a low risk activity that's different from your athletic training routine. As mundane as it might sound, dress appropriately. If it's raining or snowing, use an umbrella and wear a hat and gloves. Don't worry about looking like a "cool" athlete; be a healthy athlete!

Eat breakfast every day. Eat a balanced diet. Pay attention to your nutritional needs during training and competition. Most athletic departments have nutritionists on their medical or training staffs to help you figure out how to eat to maximize your athletic and academic potential.

Don't mess around with your health. If you're feeling run down, be sure to get plenty of rest and take extra care to boost your immunity before you actually get sick. Drink lots of fluids, especially water, orange juice, and chicken soup (yes, it really works!). Get extra sleep. If you do get sick, go to your athletic medical staff as soon as you can and follow their instructions to get better.

## 8. Stay Focused and Positive: Learn to Harness Your Competitive Spirit

The adrenaline rush in the first year of college is perhaps unequaled to any other point in one's life. The highs and lows of classes, the ups and downs of social relationships, and athletic defeats and accomplishments are as exulting as they can seem devastating.

There is the move to campus, putting your college uniform on for the first time, getting settled with your roommate, taking your first exam, writing your first paper, participating in your first athletic competition. Some days will be never-ending, seeming to go on forever and ever. And then there will be a broken relationship, a critical comment from a professor, a bad practice, a bad phone call from home, a sports injury, a rejection, a conflict with the college bureaucracy. How could it get so bad, you will wonder in your frustration and dismay. Then, before you know it, there is an invitation in the mail, an A on a quiz, a walk across campus with a new friend, a text from an old friend, or a great win. All of this and it's only the second week of college! How could this be?

College is about becoming a grown-up, intense learning and studying, independence, and the onset of adulthood. It's about the new people you are meeting, the new ideas you are confronting, and your successes and failures. Some moments are glorious and provoke highs you haven't ever felt before. Other moments are sad, depressing, and painful.

Take it one day at a time and cherish each moment (except the forgettable ones—learn from those moments and then forget them forever). Keep a journal, take pictures, store the best experiences in your permanent memory bank. List your best ideas for tomorrow and for the long term. Tomorrow will be here before you know it. Trust that you'll quickly get past the tough and trying moments. Make the good days last a lifetime, as your smile, laughter, and good ideas make the world a better place for all of us.

## 9. Find Opportunities to Get Involved Beyond Your Sport

It is very important to your success in college that you feel connected and involved in campus life. Not only is it important for your mental and emotional well-being, but it is also a central ingredient for your academic success. Students who feel a connection to their college are much more likely to do well there, to go on to graduate, and to have positive college experiences.

Being a student athlete provides an immediate and intense connection to your school. However, while you may feel connected to your college through your athletic participation, you may find it more difficult to get involved in anything besides your sport. You might feel isolated from the rest of the university, given the time demands of both your classes and your sport.

Get involved outside of your sport. Find the options that are already part of your busy schedule or that fit into your time constraints. Explore campus activities, organizations, and events. Expand your social, academic, and athletic networks. Go out of your way to meet other students in your classes and in your residence hall. Make friends with athletes on other teams.

Most colleges have learning communities whose very purpose is to create smaller, more personal learning environments involving faculty and staff. In addition, some universities today have programs that allow undergraduates, including first-year students, to participate in research with faculty. A growing number of campuses also offer course-based intergroup dialogues, which bring together two or more social identity groups to talk openly and frankly about the sometimes difficult issues between groups. See Tip 6 on pages 130–32.

Many athletic departments provide community service opportunities for their athletes to support the local community. See Tip 5 on pages 129–30. These activities can include visiting patients in the local hospitals, raising money through various activities to support charitable causes, or tutoring students in the local schools.

There are numerous campus organizations to suit your interests in areas such as politics, sports, media, art, music and theater, writing, race and ethnicity, and religion. There are also clubs for those who want to pursue their areas of study, specific graduate schools, or professions.

In addition to the option of getting involved in an organization, everyday opportunities exist to attend lectures, concerts, plays, sporting events, and many other activities. See Tip 1 on pages 100–2. Find an event to get you out of your room and into the campus community.

These wonderful opportunities will allow you to feel connected intellectually and socially to college life. Take your time and make your choices carefully so as to not over-commit yourself early on. It takes time and experience to balance your academic and athletic demands. You will have four or five years to try out these academic and social options. Don't rush to get all of this done in your first month of college.

## 10. Get to Know Your Faculty and Give Them the Chance to Know You

Getting to know faculty at your college must be one of your top priorities. It will make all the difference in your college experience. See Tip 6 on page 66–67 and Tip 8 on pages 69–71.

Don't consider yourself a successful student if you don't know at least one professor well enough to ask for advice, discuss some academic topic, and request a letter of recommendation. It is well known that students who succeed in college have good relationships with one or more faculty members.

Getting to know faculty is a special and unique opportunity. You get to spend time in their environment—in their classes, their labs, their offices, their lecture halls, their campus hangouts—during which time your primary purpose is to pursue ideas and the intellectual life. It's in this sense that college is so different from high school. These faculty members don't just come to work to teach you. They live and breathe their intellectual work 24-hours a day, and they want to have you join them in their journey during your short stay in their environment. Don't miss out!

So how do you meet a faculty member? The best approach is to take a small enough class or seminar that personal relationships naturally develop. You see the instructor a few times a week in class; he or she debates ideas with you, reads your papers, and writes back to you with insightful comments. You'll likely feel comfortable meeting with the instructor after class or during office hours.

But many of your classes won't be small seminars, so it's important to take advantage of other approaches to meet faculty. Go up to the faculty member after class and follow up on a question or idea that was raised in class. Do the same during office hours. If you're interested in the instructor's area of research, check to see if there are opportunities to be a research assistant.

You may be interested to know that there are many different ranks among the faculty. To use a football analogy, there are depth charts within the faculty ranks, but the team is comprised of the sum of all the parts. Your instructor may be a lecturer or an untenured or tenured professor at different ranks or a graduate student who may be referred to on campus as a graduate student instructor or teaching assistant. Teaching quality and interest in students varies across all the ranks.

Some colleges have mentor programs to provide structure for meeting faculty. Invite your faculty member to eat lunch with you in your residence hall, at a student union cafeteria, or at a local sandwich shop. Check with your compliance office to stay within NCAA rules. Ask your professor if he or she would be willing to speak at a meeting of some organization you're a part of. Another way to meet and talk with faculty is to join a college committee that includes students.

What should you say to your instructors when you do decide you're ready to talk with them? Ask them about themselves, about what they do, about how they got interested in their field. Ask them what they're working on now, whether it is a new research project, a journal article, a book, a community project, or a conference presentation. Tell them about a book you're reading or something you've been wondering about related to your class. Feel free to talk about any topic related directly or indirectly to the class. Tell them about your own intellectual and social interests and about your professional goals. They also will be interested to hear about your athletic accomplishments. All of these questions and topics will lead to enriching conversations and friendships that you will maintain throughout college and, in many cases, well beyond.

**CHAPTER 2**

# Make the Most of Your Opportunity: The Rules of the Game

## 1. Take Responsibility for Your Eligibility

Many student athletes start getting recruited for college scholarships as early as Grades 9 and 10. While this can be very exciting, it also makes it difficult to live in the here and now of high school. We've all heard stories about the blue-chip athlete with boxes full of recruitment letters. By the time college athletes arrive on campus to start classes, they do so with a belief that "this school really wants **me.** They fought other schools for the right to have me enroll here, and they courted me in every way possible." This kind of thinking isn't helpful to a new college student because no matter how an athlete gets to a school; he or she has to start over. It's up to you to find a way to stay.

New student athletes may not realize that once they arrive on campus, the recruitment process is over. Let it go. Regardless of what academic circumstances you find yourself in as a student athlete, you will be treated like any other student in the classroom. But your status as an athlete also subjects you to a complex and detailed set of rules imposed by athletic governing agencies—the NCAA and your conference. For example, a grade of Incomplete at the end of the term is permissible for any student, but it is usually computed as a failing grade (E or F) in determining the grade point for eligibility. Your school might even have rules for athletes that do not exist for other students, just to ensure your compliance with eligibility rules. For example, you might have to receive additional approval when dropping or adding a course to make sure that you do not lose full-time student status (12 credits).

The world of coaches is different from the world of professors, but they are more similar than it may appear on the surface. Both expect students to be respectful, committed, and responsible. Neither would consider it okay to be late or unprepared, or to miss a deadline, meeting, or assignment. Student athletes must learn to juggle their schedules and commitments with astounding proficiency.

College coaches must be concerned about academics because it is the basis of athletic eligibility, and coaches and athletic department advisors are also judged by how many of their students graduate. In fact, Division I schools use a metric called the Academic Performance Rate that holds schools accountable for academic achievement each team each term: (www.ncaa.org/wps/wcm/connect/public/NCAA/ Academics/Division+I/How+is+APR+calculated). On the other hand, professors may not even realize a particular student happens to be an athlete. This is not necessarily a positive or negative factor for that student. It does mean, however, that as a student athlete, you should not expect your professors to know you might miss class for athletic travel or, much worse, as a result of an athletic injury.

Outside of competition, you are expected to uphold your academic commitments with the same vigor as your athletic commitments. Make sure you know the protocol at your school for excused athletic absences. Check with each of your instructors about how they want you to handle these absences and make up anything you missed. There are times when travel or medical treatment might conflict with academic commitments. Be proactive in discussing this with your instructors. Do not wait to let your instructor know you will be missing class on a date that impacts other students in your class, like a group project or presentation.

Even though the amount of time athletes can practice is governed by the NCAA, it's not hard to understand the pressures involved in choices student athletes make about school versus athletics. For some of you, this may be further complicated by your dependency on athletic scholarships to attend college and the fear that if you do not meet the coach's expectations, you might jeopardize your scholarship. However, you need to remember that if you do not perform satisfactorily in the classroom, you can lose both your athletic eligibility and your academic scholarship. The lesson some college athletes learn the hard way is that being highly recruited and feeling important once upon a time does not carry any weight once you enroll as a college student.

## 2. Make Time Management Your Best Friend

An essential skill you need to develop in college is to manage your time well. This is especially important for student athletes who have two sets of demands and responsibilities. College presents you with so much unstructured time that unless you know how to organize your day, you will easily and quickly get lost. It may seem like a paradox: How can it be that the more time you have, the more likely you are to find yourself running out of time?

The answer lies in the fact that prior to coming to college, most students have led very structured lives. Your schedule was pretty much the same every day. You had classes from morning to mid or late afternoon, then you had practice and did homework, and you took part in social or extra-curricular activities in the evenings and weekends. In college you will be taking four or five classes that only meet a few times per week, leaving you with a different schedule every day and significant gaps of free time. You will be in charge of getting yourself where you need to be and on time. Your only reminders about going to sleep at a reasonable hour, when (or if) to wake up, and going to class will come from you or your alarm clock.

One key to effective time management is using a good planner. A good planner can be one of the most important tools for success in college. The trick is that you have to use it! Electronic or paper planners allow you to record all of your academic and athletic commitments. A planner works when you plan when to study and when to do your homework.

It may take you some time to discover how to plan most effectively for your study and social time. For some assignments, you may need to study in short blocks; an hour between classes then becomes an important opportunity for study and you can get a great amount accomplished. For other assignments, you may need three or four hours of uninterrupted blocks of time to really focus on a topic. If you have required times for study table or tutoring, talk with the person in charge of scheduling if you think you can study more effectively by modifying the pre-arranged schedule.

Set realistic goals for what you need to do and when in order to meet your due dates or to be ready for exams. At the beginning of each term, you will receive a course syllabus with course requirements and due dates. Enter the information you have about each of your classes from your course syllabi. Enter your athletic practices, meetings, and competition schedules, plus any other appointments and commitments. Block out time for social events and chill time. If you need reminders about eating at the right time or getting to sleep at a good time for you, include meals and bedtime too.

Many colleges and athletic departments provide students with planners, or you can simply purchase one at a campus store. Use it to help you stay on track and on schedule. Chart your academic and non-academic commitments, including structured and unstructured social time. Student athletes who are good time managers still have to make tough choices involving their classes, school work, sport, social activities, and hanging out with friends. Learning to use your time effectively means that you are more likely to make the right choices about your time and also have more time to do what you want.

Many students are familiar with using the calendars in their phones. This is a good way to note exam and other due dates, but phones and other electronic devices do not serve the same purpose as planners. Whether you use an electronic or paper planner, list your due dates, appointments, and meetings on the monthly pages, and use the weekly and daily versions to actually plan your path to meeting your deadlines. Be sure to include when and what you have to study to be prepared for an exam.

When you're working efficiently because you're well organized, you will have the gratifying feeling of accomplishing your goals for the day. You'll feel good knowing you built a schedule that allocates time for your dual academic and athletic responsibilities but also keeps you balanced socially and enables you to enjoy your friends and the full college experience. And reward yourself—you earned it!

## 3. Identify Your Academic Advising and Support Teams

Once you are in college, you will have two teams: your athletic team and your academic team. Your academic team consists of your assigned academic advisor, your athletic department academic support advisor, your instructors, and the various other individuals who provide you with additional academic support. Your athletic team consists of your coaches, the athletes on your team, and the additional staff who provide physical and medical assistance to help you perform your best.

This all sounds great, but it can be overwhelming. Who can help with what and when? What if you get different or conflicting advice? Who will really give you the right information? Advisors will want to talk with you about the classes you select, your grades, your adjustment to college, your selection of major, your degree completion plan, and how you are doing in general. If you have two advisors assigned to you, one in your school and one in athletics, learn what each advisor can and should do for you. Sometimes determining whom to go to can be difficult since you know that all of your advisors are genuinely concerned about you and your academic and athletic success.

Think of your college advisor as your academic coach whose mission is to help you grow, improve your skills, prepare you for each upcoming challenge, and achieve your goals. Some students make the mistake of maintaining distance from their advisors because they view them as rule enforcers or as the people they must see if they are in academic trouble. Others maintain distance because they did not have a good experience with their high school advisor and don't understand why they need an advisor at college. If for any reason you do not feel comfortable with your assigned advisor, it is important that you change advisors and find one with whom you can develop a good relationship.

Your academic advisor's primary mission is for you to be academically successful and to graduate from college. Advisors can be a tremendous resource for information and about which courses to take which terms and about the quality and rigor of courses and faculty. The ideal relationship is one where you and your academic advisor think together about your intellectual interests, professional goals, and life commitments. Your advisor wants you to do the necessary work of identifying and clarifying your own individual desires and goals in order to help you make the decisions about what path to choose.

Athletic department advisors are responsible for your academics as they relate to athletic eligibility. The purpose of athletic eligibility is to ensure that student athletes are making appropriate progress toward their degrees as governed by the NCAA, the school's conference, and the academic requirements of their college. While your advisors would agree on common goals, keep in mind that the advice of athletic department advisors may be more focused on concerns for your eligibility while the advice of academic advisors may be more focused on your overall degree progress and requirements. Make sure the advice you get from both sources meets all of your needs. In the best case scenario, you and your advisors will consult and work together. It is important that you have an advocate in both departments. The bottom line is that your athletic eligibility is contingent on your academic eligibility. As a student athlete (at any level), you must be academically eligible in order to be athletically eligible. If you do not do well academically, you will not be able to play/participate.

The ideal formula for student athlete advising is a triangle. Draw one in the margin now. The three points are the student, the academic unit advisor, and the athletic department advisor. Each leg of the triangle touches both of the other legs. The student is connected to both advisors and each advisor is connected to the student and the other advisor. Keep this picture in your mind as the way to make the most of the advising available to you.

In addition to your assigned advisors, you will have additional resources, including tutors, study group leaders, learning specialists, mentors, coaches, trainers, and people who can provide support for a broad variety of life and career issues. You may have various formal and informal mentors, including your parents, siblings, upper-class friends, high school coaches, mentors through your religious affiliations, and even your best friend's parents.

Consider yourself lucky to have so many people who care about you. Think carefully about whose advice to take to heart and whose advice to take with "a grain of salt." If this gets too much to manage, take advice only from your academic and athletic advisors. Don't make decisions about college academics without talking to both of them.

## 4. Follow the Rules of the Classroom

It is a common assumption that by enrolling in college, you have made a deliberate decision to enter the scholarly community of higher education and have accepted the responsibilities that are a part of that community. This means that there is an expectation that you will behave in a respectful manner to your instructors and peers and that they will be respectful toward you.

The first sign of respect is to go to class and to be on time. Particularly in a small class, you are responsible for contributing to the course's success. You cannot contribute if you do not attend. Whether you are in a small or large class, when you come to class late you disrupt and interrupt the lecture or discussion that is in progress.

Your non-verbal body language is an important indicator of how engaged you are in the class. Do not sit in class with a hat on or plugged in to an electronic device. Sit in the front of the class, and not in a pack with your teammates. Come to class alert, and be prepared to take good notes.

Turn off your cell phone during class. Do not send text messages. It's rude to everyone for you to receive calls or send text messages during class. Do not attempt to communicate with others by talking or whispering. Don't play computer games or be distracted by vibrations indicating new phone and text messages. You know about the dangers of driving while you are talking on the phone or text messaging. Doing so in the college classroom poses a high risk to your academic success and to your relationship with your professor and other students.

Only open your laptop or other electronic devices in class if your professor allows it and, if you have permission to use your laptop, stick to the assignment. Don't go online or visit social networking sites when you are supposed to be taking notes in class. Would you like it if you were speaking during class and your instructor was not paying attention because he or she was reading email messages? Or, if during your class presentation, your fellow students were reading newspapers, sending texts, or doing crossword puzzles? This is not respectful or acceptable classroom behavior, so do not allow yourself to adopt such bad habits.

Don't sleep during class. If you are so tired that you can't stay awake, it's useless for you to be there. No one wants you there when you are sleeping. You might have practice or workouts before class. If you think you will get drowsy, take an ice cold drink with you to sip on.

Be a respectful student and member of the higher education learning community. Get yourself mentally situated to be engaged in the learning process the moment class starts. Be ready to ask questions and to offer analyses and insights. Practice good listening skills. Get to know the professor as well as your fellow classmates.

It is a privilege to attend college. First-generation college students are always among the most respectful students in class. They seem to have a special appreciation for the power and privilege that are captured in the opportunity to be part of a scholarly community at an institution of higher learning. They are joined by most of their classmates in that respectful behavior. Be a member of this respectful majority, and never forget how fortunate you are.

## 5. Make Good Choices: Follow the Rules

Being a college student and living on a college campus comes with new-found independence. You are often in the position of making many of your own decisions for the first time in your life. You will have both tremendous freedom and tremendous responsibility at the same time. In the college student part of your life, it's easy to think that you can do just about anything you want just about anytime. It's your decision to go to class or sleep in, go to the library or meet up with your friends, work on your project or go to a movie. Your parents may remain a constant in your life via cell phones and email, but they are not physically in the same place with you to closely monitor or influence your behavior.

You've been learning right from wrong throughout your life in preparation for this time when you must make your own decisions. As a young independent adult and a college student athlete, the stakes will be higher than they were in high school, but you will know the right and wrong choice in almost every case. Making the right choices is often the difference between success and failure in college. *But the message here is that you do not need to learn the right thing to do—you already know it.* The challenge for most college students is making the leap from *knowing the right decision* to *acting on the right decision.* Just knowing the right thing to do is not enough; you actually have to *do* it. That might sound easy enough, but there will be many forces pulling you in the wrong direction.

Mature, adult decision-making is the difference between doing what you want to do and doing what you should do. Working on your project or going out with friends? There will be many opportunities for you to make decisions every day. Learn to distinguish between the important ones and the less significant ones. If you make the wrong choice, you will be the one to suffer the consequences. Learn from your mistakes. Promise yourself not to repeat the same mistake; otherwise, you have not learned anything.

In college you will be treated as an adult and be held accountable for your choices and decisions. This is something many students have not yet experienced. If you are not sure what to do, play out the various scenarios in your mind. What is the best case and worst case if you choose option A or option B? It might help to talk it over with someone whose opinion you trust, like a good friend, mentor, advisor, instructor, coach, or parent.

In stark contrast to your life as a college student, your life as a college athlete imposes more structure and more rules than high school athletics. You are strictly bound to adhere to a vast number of rules and regulations imposed by the NCAA and your conference. You should be briefed on these rules by staff in your athletic department, but it is ultimately your responsibility. As you know from media coverage of various scandals in college athletics, players who ignore or disregard the rules will get themselves, their coaches, their teams, and their schools in trouble with the NCCA.

Given the demands and rules of college athletics, living on your own may offer too much independence and leave too much to chance. In the end, you are left with this dichotomy of almost complete independence in one sphere of your new life and more structure and rules than you ever had before in the other sphere. The more intense the heat is athletically, the more you might be tempted to get some relief by doing things you think you can get away with in the short run, like skipping class or not turning in assignments. You know, of course, that it will all catch up with you, but on the day you really want to sleep in or go to a party, it might not feel like something you want to worry about. *We want you to worry and to go to class. That is the right decision.*

Always make good choices for yourself. You know the right thing to do.

**Jean Stone: "Pat your head and rub your tummy."**

*Having lettered in varsity soccer, track, and water polo in high school, Jean Stone had a lot of experience with coaches. She knew how to act and what to expect. But she came to college in awe of her professors. After all, hadn't all the college admissions literature talked about how smart, articulate, and renowned the professors were? She had held her high school teachers in high regard, and while some of them were truly excellent, she felt like there were some who just didn't know what they were talking about. Her college professors had PhDs and wrote books; those sure seemed credentials enough to Jean.*

*Jean also believed what she read in textbooks. Weren't you supposed to? She couldn't even imagine that textbooks could have a particular perspective, hold a certain point of view, or even be wrong. It all seemed pretty straightforward to Jean; you go to college to study with brilliant professors and learn all about your major from informative texts.*

*Jean's experience with her coaches certainly proved out that assumption about believing what textbooks and professors tell you. On all her teams, the coach's word was Truth. It was not the athlete's role to question the coach, just to trust and follow. Even though Jean and her teammates would occasionally grumble in the locker room or second-guess a decision here and there, they all trusted and believed in their coaches. After all, a team doesn't go far if it doesn't give its coach its full effort and trust. Besides, Jean still shuddered when she* remembered her high school coach humiliating her in front of her teammates when she had raised a question that her coach took as a direct challenge to his authority.

Jean's first weeks of college went just as she had expected. The professor handed out a clear and sensible syllabus, readings were assigned, and homework and tests were scheduled throughout the semester. In science class one day, the professor had students turn to page 40 of their textbook and asked students what they thought of the information and explanation presented. The students were mostly quiet, except for those few who always raised their hands. But the professor wasn't satisfied with their comments—she said that there was an alternative explanation that challenged what the text was presenting as fact. Jean was surprised that the textbook wouldn't be up-to-date, but she thought that this just showed how brilliant her professor was. Students discussed the alternative explanation and offered a variety of comments to demonstrate why it now seemed preferable to the textbook information.

Then the professor said that she didn't accept the alternative explanation either. And, further, she stated that she didn't have a good explanation of either of those that had been presented thus far, but that this confusion was exactly what made science interesting to her. Jean's classmates were confused—of all her classes, science had been the most clear, definitive, and unquestioned. Jean was now very confused. She could not imagine her coach would have admitted to not knowing something because he was supposed to know everything about his sport and she really believed he did. This really threw her.

In her psychology class, Jean thought she did perfectly on her first paper. She had carefully read the texts for class and taken copious notes. But the professor in that class wrote all over her paper asking Jean why she believed what she had written. The professor wanted to know why Jean just accepted different authors' opinions as fact. Hadn't Jean heard the professor challenge the authors' theories and perspectives? The professor wanted Jean's opinion, and he also wanted Jean to be able to make strong arguments to support her point of view.

This was all new to Jean. In sports, she knew to do exactly what the coach told her and not to question, challenge, or think for herself. This approach had always worked very well for her. She knew full well from personal experience that anyone who didn't follow the coach's instructions or rules would end up doing laps and push-ups and all kinds of nasty chores.

At first, Jean found it terribly difficult to go from following instructions at water polo practice to being a questioning student in the classroom. It was confusing, like patting your head and rubbing your tummy at the same time. It made her feel a little dizzy. And, she wondered whether one approach was really better than the other. On the way home from practice, Jean whispered to her teammate, "I don't get it. Are my professors goofy or is Coach just a tyrant?"

After a while, though, Jean realized that she didn't need to be so single-minded. She came to see the value in both approaches and learned how to adapt to both the athletic and academic cultures. By becoming more flexible, she was able to succeed at different ways of learning and gained a set of intercultural competencies that few of *her peers had achieved. In class she let her inquisitive, creative, and analytical side flourish, and while she walked to practice she learned to switch gears to her "athletic mindset," which enabled her to follow the coach's rules without the type of questioning she was learning to do in her classes.*

*Jean was proud of herself for figuring out this puzzle and considered it to be one of her best lessons learned at college. She realized that her new adaptability and her flexibility and skill in learning in different ways would be a tremendous benefit to her not only in college, but likely would serve her well throughout her adult life.*

## 6. Return to the Three Rs: Reading, 'Riting, and 'Rithmetic

Now that you've been admitted to college, you may be feeling both very confident in your academic abilities and at the same time embarrassed that you still need help with some of the basic fundamental learning skills. Far too many students, both those from weak high schools as well as those from high schools considered the best in the country, still need some instruction and support in one or more areas of the basics. This is true for *all* students. Be sure to get this additional instruction and support. Do not rely on trying to take courses that seem easier to avoid confronting your academically weak areas. Your courses will become increasingly more difficult, so it is important to strengthen your basic skills. Otherwise, it will become more and more difficult to perform well academically.

Even more distressing than the fact that too many students have inadequate skills in the basics is that there is shame associated with this. Students far too often will try to hide their lacking skills in these areas, and faculty far too often do not challenge students to get the instructional support they need.

You are a smart and educated person, so why haven't you learned these skills? In some cases, the K–12 schools or teachers did not provide the basic educational foundation needed. In other cases, students may have successfully hidden their need for additional educational support while in high school. In still other cases, educational policy in some well-intentioned schools may have tipped too far to emphasize broader themes of learning and the basic skills did not receive sufficient emphasis. Regardless of the reason, however, you can learn all of these skills. In fact, because you are in college, almost all of which have numerous kinds of academic resource centers and support services, you have a unique opportunity now to learn these skills and develop them. Student athletes also have the advantage of academic support programs that are located within athletic departments. Don't try to use your smarts to hide something you did not learn in high school: Get help!

Some athletes are intimidated to ask for help because they feel more visible than non-athletes. But keep in mind that you will be respected for taking your education seriously and for embracing your educational as well as your athletic opportunities. After you graduate from college, you may never have the chance or the inclination to go back to these areas of inadequate skills. If you feel bad enough now to hide the areas in which you know you need help, you will feel worse after college, assuming your skill deficiencies do not impede your ability to stay in college. Now is the time to ask for help.

If you find yourself needing help, let go of any negative feelings, low self-image, or embarrassment for asking. This is not a test of your intellectual ability—these are skills! Give yourself an emotional break with this.

Go online or talk to your advisors, your instructors, or your friends and find out where the academic resources are located. And be patient. It may take some time to fully learn these skills. Finally, go on with your life and enjoy! Know that ensuring you have a strong educational foundation will help you be successful in college and beyond.

## 7. Learn to Balance Your Academic and Athletic Responsibilities

Both your academic and athletic commitments will increase in the transition from high school to college.

The consequences of not maintaining these new and more intense commitments differs between academics and athletics. Academic consequences are often longer term and have a cumulative affect. For instance, skipping class will negatively affect how you perform on your exams and papers and that, in turn, will ultimately impact your final grade. In athletics, if you miss or are late for practice, meetings, or treatment, you will most likely receive immediate consequences from your coach, but it may not likely have a long-term impact. Ultimately, not doing what you should be doing academically and/or athletically will affect both you and your team.

The responsibility to fully meet your dual commitments is up to you. To stay on top of both, you will have to be disciplined and sometimes make tough choices about your time. This is a common problem for student athletes. Talk to your advisors and the upper-class students on your team who seem to have figured it out. You will probably conclude that you will have to give up some of your social or leisure time.

Keep track of how you spend your time. Detail how much of each day is required for academics, athletics, meals, sleep, and social time. You will be surprised at how much time you have during the day that goes unaccounted for or that could be more productive, giving you more free time to relax and socialize.

Student athletes are competitive by nature and, as a result, some fall into the trap of making the choice to overextend their academic or athletic commitments. For instance, in academics, some student athletes feel they can never study enough. These students need to learn to study effectively and to judge when they are no longer studying productively. In athletics, their competitive nature often compels them to put in more practice or training time than required, especially before a big game or meet or if a teammate seems to be moving in on their position. As you become more proficient at managing your time, you will end up having more time for everything that is important to you.

Communication is the best approach if you are having difficulty managing your commitments. If you are late for class because of an athletic commitment or if you are late for practice because of an academic commitment, explain to the coach or instructor that you are doing your best to balance your commitments and ask for support. Give them specific examples of the dilemma(s) you face and what steps you will take to prevent the same occurrence from happening in the future. You will likely earn their respect for trying to be responsible, and you may find that they will be more accommodating than you would expect. If that doesn't work, your academic and athletic advisors should also be able to assist you in addressing your conflict.

## 8. Learn How You Learn

Not every student learns in the same way. Along the path of your 12 years of formal education, you may have observed that you, your friends, and other students in your classes absorb, process, and retain information differently. You can be a more successful student if you understand your own learning style.

Do you understand new concepts best when they are presented verbally, visually (on the board, as handouts, etc.), or both? Can you listen and take notes at the same time, or do you miss what the teacher is saying or can't figure out what you wrote in your notes? You should be able to answer these learning input questions because you know better than anyone how you learn best. But up until now, you may not have been proactive about using this information to your benefit.

Identify how you learn best and maximize your learning by adapting to your individual style. If your instructor only lectures without visual aids or if you need a verbal addition to enhance your reading comprehension, explore how you can adapt the delivery of information in your courses to your own learning style. You should be able to get help with this from academic support offices on campus.

Taking notes is very important because how you take notes will determine how successfully you can study for exams. Ask somebody to evaluate your note-taking skills. There are reasonably priced kits on the market that have recorders built into pens that enable you to record lectures while you take notes and then match the notes to the lecture. There is also computer software that scans your readings so you can improve your comprehension while reading off a computer screen. Find out what resources are available on your campus, at bookstores, and on the Internet.

In addition to being aware of learning inputs, you should gain expertise in learning outputs. As you know from your extensive experience in school, an important component of being a successful student is being able to demonstrate that you have learned the material through quizzes, papers, exams, projects, and class participation. How good are your test-taking skills? You want to be aware of how well you perform on different kinds of exams, such as short answer, fill in the blank, multiple choice, or essay exams.

In our experience, students who excel in performance areas such as art, music, dance, and athletics often learn and demonstrate what they have learned in ways that are different from other students. (This phenomenon is sometimes associated with differences between dominance of the right brain versus the left brain.) It is not unusual for student athletes to feel they earn better grades on papers and essay exams than short answer, true and false, or multiple choice exams. This kind of information should never be the sole criteria for course selection. It is necessary to become skilled at learning in different ways, but, mostly, it is important to figure out how you learn and test so you can benefit from that knowledge sooner rather than later. As an athlete, your academic performance is regulated beginning with your first term on campus. You do not have the luxury of time that non-athletes often have to figure these things out.

You want to be evaluated on what you know, not on whether you know how to take multiple choice or true/false tests. A major aspect of the preparation for standardized tests is learning the process of how to take the test. This is true for exams you will take in college, too.

What are your communication and class participation skills? Do you love to get involved in class discussions or do you freeze when the instructor calls on you?

Most course descriptions include information about the assignments and requirements for the course. While these should not be the sole criteria for course selection, pay attention to those factors that will make a difference in your grade.

Strategize so you can maximize both your learning input and output strengths and skills. It will be well worth the time and effort.

## 9. Be Intellectually Honest: Don't Cheat

Academic integrity is the academic equivalent of civil law. Academic integrity is essential to the entire enterprise of scholarly inquiry and intellectual exploration. Cheating is stealing ideas, thoughts, and somebody's else's academic work. If you are caught cheating, you will be brought before an academic judiciary. You will face punishment that can range from a stern warning to a failing grade on a test or on an entire course, or even suspension or expulsion.

The best and only advice about cheating is to never, ever do it. Your purpose in college is to learn, and you will learn nothing from cheating. You are stealing from someone else in order to get a better grade. And the penalty of being caught will always exceed the penalty of not cheating in the first place.

There are different views as to why cheating has increased on college campuses. Some people believe it reflects the breakdown of basic values in society, a lack of respect for rules, peers, and authority. Others suggest that there is so much stress and competition to get top grades, particularly in the pre-professional programs, that students feel pressured to break the rules in order to fulfill their professional goals. Finally, some students unknowingly cheat, not being fully aware of what constitutes plagiarism.

Students cheat—and get caught—in any number of high-tech and low-tech ways. They look over a classmate's shoulder during an exam to get an answer, or they copy other students' papers or buy papers over the Internet. They use other people's work without giving citations or set up computer programs to use other people's work for lab assignments and math problems. Faculty and university administrators know all the tricks of the trade and are quite adept at identifying student cheaters.

The question of academic integrity is a matter of personal integrity. The cheating habits you develop or maintain in college are likely to stay with you throughout your business life and personal relations. If you cheat because you feel unbearable stress in college, rest assured that the pressure will be that much more intense and stressful in the work world. Don't start down this path. You are better than this. You don't want or need to get ahead by cheating. It will never feel as good as getting ahead because you deserve it based on your own accomplishments.

As a student athlete, you may feel pressure because you are running out of time or because you need to meet certain standards for your athletic eligibility. But remember how much you have at stake. You can lose your scholarship and your athletic eligibility if you are caught cheating. It is always better to turn in an assignment late or not answer a question on an exam than it is to cheat. Most instructors will accept late papers with a deduction of points for being late. Talk to your instructors; they may be willing to give you an extension, especially if you were sick, injured, or away for an excused athletic competition.

Live your life honestly so you can be proud of all your accomplishments. Examine your ethical makeup and your personal integrity. Set yourself on the right course in college, and it will serve you well throughout your entire life.

## 10. Anticipate and Prepare for Setbacks

Life happens, whether or not you are a student, athlete, or both. College does not exist in a vacuum for anyone. Despite your best attempts to manage your schedule and take care of yourself, events will occur that result in setbacks in your academic and athletic lives. These events can include problems with your family, finances, or roommates. They can include illness, injuries, breakdowns with your car or your technology, and other unpredictable occurrences. Since you won't always know when something is going to happen or how it will affect you, keep yourself in a position to diffuse and minimize such interferences and distractions.

There are several important strategies that will minimize the impact of life's unexpected events. These include being well organized, using your planner to keep up with your work and assignments, and not procrastinating or leaving work until the last minute. Staying current with your school work is key. You stand a better chance of catching up if you are not behind when something unexpected happens.

Another important strategy is to know how and where to get the information you might need when you need it. What if your computer crashes or you're too sick to go to class? Familiarize yourself with the resource materials you are given at new student orientation and those provided on your school's website. When you need to take action, you will have a better starting point.

Adverse situations that can cause setbacks academically and athletically fall into two categories—those affecting you directly and those for which you feel some responsibility to fix. You will have more control in those situations that affect you directly. It is also reasonable to believe you can do what is necessary to resolve the problem at hand. Those affecting family members, close friends, or people you care about may be problems you want to fix, but the fix is likely out of your hands. For example, if you are sick, you know what to do to get better. You can contact your instructors regarding work you are missing and plan how to catch up. But if one of your immediate family members falls ill, you may be torn about staying at school or going home to be with your family. You will be faced with balancing your need to stay focused on school and your sport with your desire to be with your family. In these situations, hold true to your priorities, values, and beliefs. Only you can really understand the dynamics of the situation and the best course of action for you.

Don't assume you are expected to manage life crises on your own now because you're in college. Talk to the people who can help you. Let your instructors, advisors, and coaches know what's going on. They may be able to help in ways you hadn't thought about. If you need help, get help, and if you're not sure how or where, go to someone you trust. Seek advice—and the sooner, the better. Being a mature, responsible adult means being smart enough to get help when you need it. Lucky for you, there are many people at your college ready to help you!

# 3

# Seek Advice and Learn to Listen: Practice Hard and Make Use of the Training Room

## 1. Be a Learner, Not Just a Student

The essence of being a learner is to be an active participant in your education. It's easy to go through the motions of being a student. You just have to "talk the talk"—go to class, take notes, go to study table, do the homework, etc. Being a learner, however, requires the investment of going to class prepared, doing the readings, taking meaningful notes and reviewing your notes after lecture, participating in a study group to have several minds to challenge others' ideas, and meeting with your instructor during office hours. To be a learner, you have to "walk the walk"—you have to do the maximum instead of the minimum.

You can relate to this using an athletic analogy, as well. There is a clear difference between the team meetings, practices, drills, and training that you do when you are 100 percent focused and committed versus the days you just want to get in and get out or are distracted by something else on your mind.

Learning to be a learner will be a new experience in each class. It will be up to you to assess the professor, the syllabus, the course content, and the requirements to figure out what you can do to learn as much as possible from that specific class. This may sound like extra work, but it will make your life easier in the long run. The more you put into your education, the more you will get out of it.

In your college classroom, as in your life journey, it is also time to ask hard questions. Challenge your professors about what they tell you as fact or what they offer as interpretation. How did they come to that opinion? Look for the evidence and the research behind their analysis. Do the careful reading that is essential to asking good questions. Challenge the authors that you read. Become a critical and serious thinker. Be thoughtful in your self reflection, and be critical in your questioning of the ideas, assertions, and analyses that others pose to you. Evaluate what you read and what you hear without bias. It is a good time to challenge yourself as well. Challenge your prior assertions, stereotypes, and conclusions.

Embrace the opportunity to explore your intellectual world. Think back to the wonder of a three-year-old who asks why about everything. Approach your college learning with that same sense of wonder and excitement.

## 2. Master Studying for Exams

Many students come to college without knowing the best way to study for exams or how to take exams. It is not unusual for students to earn lower grades on their first set of college exams than they were used to getting in high school. The explanation we hear most frequently from students is that the breadth and depth of information college instructors expect on exams far exceeds the high school standard.

Exam preparation is the foundation for doing well on exams. What is the best way to prepare? Believe it or not, the best way to prepare for exams is to honor the common sense of how your brain works. You retain the most information the soonest after you receive it. The advice you've heard over the years but probably ignored, about reviewing your notes right after class is absolutely true.

Develop a system that enables you to review the notes you take each day. If your notes are sketchy or incomplete, you will be able to fill them in while the lecture is still fresh in your mind. During your study time, it is well worth spending time each day reviewing your notes for each class. As the term progresses and you have more notes for each class, you can review half your classes one day and the other half the next day. The trick is to be sure you keep reviewing your notes from the very beginning of the term so when you are studying for exams during the term or for the final exam you are not reading your notes for the first time. This process of ongoing review makes it much easier to study and retain information over the course of the semester.

This approach may sound like a lot of extra work for you and, as a result, you may find it easy to put off. But making this a routine part of your study time will pay off exponentially in terms of learning and grades and, surprisingly, will ultimately reduce the amount of time you need to study for exams. Like any good habit, it is better to make use of it as often as you can rather than not do it at all. Reviewing lecture notes is also an excellent use for the small pockets of time that you might otherwise waste during the day.

When you are studying for a specific exam, start by creating a study timeline. Use your planner to pace your study time with a peak performance date in mind, the same way you would plan for a peak athletic performance. This method also makes it harder to procrastinate. Try not to learn the hard way that cramming for exams the way you might have done in high school will simply not work in college. There is just too much information and too high of an expectation for your learning. Not waiting until the last minute to study also gives you the opportunity to find out what you don't understand so you can meet with your instructors, if needed, and make better use of your tutors and study groups.

## 3. Use Your Academic Resources

Colleges encourage all students to take advantage of available academic resources. These often include labs for math and sciences, especially chemistry and physics, and language labs where students can get help with oral and written language skills. English departments usually have help centers where you can meet with a writing tutor to work on a paper for any subject. Some academic departments even have free peer tutors—often undergraduates who have done well in the courses they are tutoring. Of course, you can always find a tutor for pay in any subject on any campus.

Your instructors should always be the first people you talk with when you need help understanding something from a lecture or an assignment. Instructors often comment that student athletes do not go to their office hours often enough because they depend more on available tutoring through the athletic department. This may also be the result of office hours conflicting with athletic commitments. If you can't make your instructors' office hours, try to schedule an alternate time. Most instructors are more than happy to make accomodations for students who cannot make their office hours.

Keep in mind that there are both general academic resources and more individualized academic resources for students who require more specific and intensive academic support.

Your first step should be to figure out whether your questions or difficulties lie in the actual course content or in the foundational background you are expected to have for your course. This information will help you determine where and what kind of help you need for a given course. For example, if your difficulty with physics is because you can't do the math, you might be better off going to the math lab than getting help from a physics tutor. Each situation and each individual student athlete is different; begin by talking with your instructor or your advisors to figure out what you need.

To make the most of your tutoring session, come prepared with specific questions about the lecture, assignments, and work you have already attempted to complete on your own. The tutor cannot help you without understanding the specific difficulty you are having with the reading, the problem set, or the concepts from the lecture. If you don't think you and the tutor are a good match, switch tutors. You might do better with a tutor who has a different approach.

The high achieving, smart students on campus do well in college by taking full advantage of the academic resources and tutors that are available. Be one of those high achieving, smart students!

## 4. Don't Fall Behind: You're Too Busy to Let This Happen

Time will play tricks with your mind at the start of college. You will think that you have loads of free time for studying. You will be surprised in the first weeks of the semester that some professors teaching subjects such as math and chemistry are reviewing material that you already covered in high school. You will take heart that only a few papers are required in any given social science or humanities course over the entire semester.

"What's the big deal," you will think. College does not seem as difficult as you always heard about. Instead of studying, you may choose to fill your time with extra-curricular activities, clubs, socializing in the residence hall, watching lots of TV, playing video games, or putting extra time into your sport.

Then—and it will seem like it hits all of a sudden—the pace will change dramatically. The first exams will be held. The first set of papers will be due. Instead of review, your professors will begin covering new material two or three times as fast as you ever learned anything in high school. In each class you will be reading entire books in a week and multiple, high-level academic articles for each class session.

How will you keep up when the semester shifts into warp speed? The answer is simple: You will need to have the best traits of both the tortoise and the hare. You need to be steady and consistent in your study habits and ready for the long haul of the semester. At the same time, you also need to be ready for the bursts of energy required when there is an especially heavy load of tests or papers assigned in any given week. That won't happen often, but it will happen at least once each term, so it's best to keep yourself in good mental and physical health for those times when you need to set everything aside to get all your work done.

The key is to always keep up with your work, even when the workload seems light. Falling behind and catching up later should never be an option. It might have worked in high school, but it won't work in college. By keeping up with your work, you will be in good shape when a rush of assignments from multiple classes are all due at once. It will allow you the much needed flexibility for those times when you catch a cold, have heavy athletic or other extra-curricular commitments, or something very exciting comes up spontaneously.

Generations of college student athletes have been able to keep up with heavy workloads. You can do this, too. You have the ability and experience to be successful. Just remember that it takes more time to catch up when you're behind than it does to keep up each day along the way. Avoid falling behind.

## 5. Ask Questions

Ever since first grade, teachers have been telling you that there is no such thing as a bad question. Yet you know in your heart that they didn't really mean it. For as soon as those words would come out of your teacher's mouth, some innocent, believing student in class would raise his or her hand and then get ridiculed for asking just that—a bad question.

We urge you to lose your fear of asking a bad question before you come to college. Chances are good that you are not the only person with that question, and if you are not planning to ask questions, and lots of them, you might as well not be in college.

Questioning is at the core of intellectual life at a university. It comes from basic human curiosity. Its source is our need to explore what isn't yet understood, to discover the unknown, to examine the truths behind the truth, and to develop the capacity to see from multiple perspectives. Questioning allows our social and scientific worlds to advance from one generation to the next.

Asking questions is also a very practical matter. You need to know where your class is going to be held so you can be there on time on the first day of class. You need to know whether classes start on the hour, on the half hour, or ten minutes past the hour. You want to know how to address your professors, by their title or by their first name. You need to know when your first exam is due, what your professor thinks about using websites as sources for research papers, and how to handle your excused absences due to athletic travel. You most certainly will need to ask how to access the rich virtual and print resources of your library.

Similarly, in your personal life, you might need to learn how to do your laundry. You will need to learn where the public bathrooms are throughout the campus. You will need to know what to do when you're standing in the hall in your towel after taking a shower and you realize you've locked yourself out of your residence hall room.

In your athletic life you will need to know the details and logistics of your scholarship or, if you are not on scholarship, how you might be able to eventually become a scholarship athlete. You will also need to know the rules about boosters and the procedures to follow if you sustain an athletic injury.

Questioning is also political. Asking the question is a statement that you have the right and the responsibility to question authorities and to question authority. You have the right to ask the department chair why your professor does not hold office hours or frequently misses classes. You have the responsibility to ask the president of your college why the faculty does not include more women who have tenure. You have the right to challenge the news media's depiction of current events. You have the responsibility to ask students at your lunch table in the residence hall cafeteria why they are laughing at racist jokes. You have the responsibility to ask why more students are not voting in campus elections for student leaders or in national presidential and congressional elections.

It's true that some questions will irritate, agitate, and complicate your life and others' lives. But that doesn't mean that the questions are bad ones. Just keep asking your questions—that's the role of the scholar.

**Jessica Wright: "Tutoring is for all students."**

*Jessica is taking the pre-business curricular track. She has always known that she would be good in business, and her parents have always encouraged and assumed that this would be her career. In addition to all her gymnastic competitions, her dad had set up summer internships in business for her during high school, and Jessica loved to follow the stock market in the daily newspaper.*

*Jessica started off her first semester with a course load that included calculus and economics. The first few weeks of math class were mostly review from high school, and Jessica felt very confident about her academic preparation and performance. She only needed to study a couple nights a week to stay on pace with the course.*

*All of a sudden, or so it seemed, the course picked up steam. The material the professor began to cover was all new to Jessica, and the problem sets were quite difficult. And there were so many of them! Jessica was used to just studying a few hours per week on each subject, and in the past her academic talent had allowed her to put in all the practice time she needed in the gym. What Jessica began to realize early in the semester was that she didn't have the study habits she needed for college. Within two weeks time with the new material, Jessica realized that she was falling way behind, and she became concerned that her first major test was coming up the next week.*

*Jessica had always been an A or B student. She had never received lower than a B in high school. Yet, on her first test, Jessica got a C-,* having missed all of the questions on material she had not already learned in high school. Jessica was embarrassed to say anything to anyone about getting help because she never had to seek help in high school. In fact, she had been a math tutor in high school. Jessica began to worry in earnest that all her plans for being both a student athlete and pursuing a career in business were not going to be realized.

After the first test, Jessica couldn't help but observe that many other students were upset about their grades. Although people were grousing about the professor and how she should have explained the material better, a few students mentioned that they were going to participate in study groups. Jessica's academic advisor had encouraged Jessica early on to join a study group and make use of the tutors that were available but, until, now, she had resisted.

Her advisor said something that stuck in her mind. "Jessica, you're a very good student and also a talented gymnast. In gymnastics, you don't think twice about getting as much help as possible from coaches, trainers, and clinics. Why do you think your academics should be any different? If you want to reach your academic potential, then, just like gymnastics, you need to take advantage of every opportunity and support service available to you to learn, study, excel, and get to the next level academically."

Jessica decided to sign up for one of the athletic department study groups. When she attended her first meeting, she recognized that there were all levels of students present. Some of the students she didn't think were very motivated, but she also knew that others were the absolute stars of the class and had actually received A grades on the exam. She was surprised to see such a mix of students there—athletes from hockey, football, tennis, golf, track, and water polo. During the study session, a number of students spoke of meeting the instructor during office hours to get help on certain questions. Others mentioned that they were also going to the math department's math lab for extra assistance.

All of this was entirely new to Jessica. Yes, she had read about the math lab in the course syllabus. And, yes, she knew her teacher consistently invited students to office hours. But Jessica had always thought that going for help was not for people like her. She decided to give it a try because she knew she had to do better on her exams.

Jessica started taking advantage of all of these resources—office hours, math lab, and the study group. It wasn't as bad as she thought, and no one stigmatized her for asking for help. In fact, she got lots of positive reinforcement from her friends and parents, and even her coach, for her effort and interest. The biggest challenge for Jessica was managing her time, which she had always been able to do well, but now she really had to keep to her schedule, especially during gymnastics season.

Jessica found that she was starting to pick up the new material and had a group of friends on other teams who shared the same struggle as her. Jessica's confidence and determination got a big boost from all of this work, and she started to feel again that she could achieve her goals. In gymnastics, she was realizing her personal best performance. And, on her next exam, Jessica got a B+ and on her final she got an A-.

# 6. Make Effective Use of Office Hours

It is very important to visit your instructors during office hours. Consider it a regular part of your routine during the first few weeks of classes and throughout the term.

Most students come to office hours right after an exam to complain about their grades or to get help with what went wrong. Those are reasonable things to talk about with your professor, and you should definitely ask them. However, those discussions are pretty routine and typical for most faculty. If that is the only time you go to office hours, it will be harder to build a relationship.

Other students come to the instructor just before an upcoming exam or paper. But if you come just before the assignment due date, you're likely to be rushed through your meeting because you'll be waiting in line with lots of your classmates. Once again, this is another good reason to see the professor, but it won't likely be a relationship builder.

The best time to visit office hours is during those times in the semester when there is no imminent paper or exam. You should just stop by, and be prepared to ask and talk about one of the course readings or topics. If you have some background on the topic, share that with the professor. You might also want to ask your instructor about his or her broader interest and experience in the field. Find out more about what professors do in their lives, what their interests are, and what projects they're currently working on. This could be helpful if you might want to do research or an independent project with this instructor in the future.

Your professor will help guide this discussion and will take an interest in you. Even if it doesn't seem that way at first, you might be surprised one day when the professor stops you on the way out of class and follows up on your earlier conversation. If you go back to the professor's office that next week or the week after, you're likely to have twice the impact and twice the possibility of building an ongoing relationship.

Think of your instructor's turf as your turf: The entire college is your academic learning environment. You have a right and responsibility to feel at home in all the academic departments where you are taking classes. Faculty hold office hours precisely to meet with students in their classes; it's not the time they set aside to do research or other intellectual work. It is the time they set aside for you. Part of what they appreciate about their lives as professors is the opportunity to engage with interesting students, just like you. Use that time wisely.

## 7. Make Appointments and Keep Them

Scheduling appointments with instructors and advisors is one of those "out of the box" transitions from high school to college. In high school, it was easier to see and speak with your instructors and advisors before, during, and after class. Their offices were usually very close to the classroom and everybody was in the same building pretty much the same hours during the day, every day. Life is very different for students who attend college and for the people who work at one.

Face-to-face communication with faculty and advisors is almost always better than email or phone. Your schedule will be full with many responsibilities, but if the answer you want to anything is yes, you are much more likely to get that answer in person.

Almost all colleges require instructors to have scheduled office hours to meet with students. Your course syllabus (outline) will include information about when and where you can meet with your instructors. Find out how to best schedule appointments through email, an assistant, online, etc. Some instructors also require individual student meetings as part of their course requirement. If you cannot attend scheduled office hours or an additional meeting time, ask to make an alternative appointment. Instructors are usually accommodating because they want to meet with students.

College advising offices usually schedule appointments online, by phone, or both. Many also have walk-in advising. Find out how often your advisor thinks you should meet and schedule those appointments in advance. If something comes up before then, you should be able to meet pretty quickly with your own advisor, or another advisor, in his or her office.

Once you schedule an appointment, it is essential that you keep it for two reasons: First, as a courtesy and, second, because you need the benefit of the conversation you had intended to have with the person with whom you scheduled the appointment. If something comes up and you cannot make the appointment or, even if you are running late, be sure to notify the individuals with as much advance notice as possible. Be considerate of other's time. Don't assume someone is just sitting in an office waiting to meet with you.

As a college student athlete, it may feel that you are busier than everyone else and that your time is more valuable. But remember that most people, whether students, faculty, or advisors, feel exactly the same way.

## 8. Choose Good Teachers over Good Class Topics

Always choose the best teacher when you are planning your class schedule. Course topics and descriptions will catch your attention, especially in college, when you will have hundreds or even thousands of courses to choose from each semester. Course topics are without a doubt important; however, a good teacher will always trump a good course title or description.

A good teacher will make any topic interesting and any course a worthwhile experience for you. You can get information and read about any topic or idea at any time. But an experience with a really good teacher—and especially a great teacher—will stay with you throughout your life, and you want to take full advantage of this opportunity.

Good teachers force you to think and learn. They will be demanding of you, they will expect you to contribute to the success of the class and come to class prepared each day, and they will be available and accessible to you. They will be interested in what you are learning from the class.

In fact, you should make a careful distinction between those faculty who stand out as good entertainers or who are popular because their classes are said to be less demanding and those who are truly good teachers. Sometimes you may want to sit back in lectures and be entertained, or you may want to balance a course load with either heavy quantitative lab work or reading/writing assignments with one from another category. Good teachers will certainly help make learning interesting, stimulating, and enjoyable, but they may not be entertainers, and they will very likely require you to think and work hard.

When you enroll in a course with an interesting topic and description, it may work out just fine for you. But savvy students talk with peers, older students, teammates, advisors, and even other faculty to find out more about the course or the professor. Some colleges post teaching evaluations of faculty and courses on student government websites. Some larger introductory courses on topics such as chemistry, statistics, psychology, and history are taught every semester by different faculty, so it might make sense to wait a semester until you can take the subject with the best instructor. But as a student athlete, you have to balance this information with your athletic requirements for normal progress toward a degree. The time frame for meeting student athlete eligibility requirements does not always allow for making choices based on one criterion over another, but careful planning with your advisor can help you maximize your options.

With good teachers, you will learn new content areas, you will be challenged to think deeply, and you will be asked to examine issues analytically and from multiple perspectives. You will be expected to do your best work, and you will want to do that because of the high standards that the professors hold for you and for themselves. You should take this opportunity to meet these professors through classroom interactions and at office hours and get to know them throughout the semester.

When you enroll in a class with a good faculty member who is also teaching a course topic you're interested in, you have a double bonus. Count on it!

## 9. Schedule Your Classes Thoughtfully and Strategically

It's a pretty amazing experience—one day you start college, and the next day you graduate, or so it seems on Graduation Day. How does that happen? What do you do along the way? How do you get from Point A to Point Z in the college game? It starts with your classes.

Classes are the foundation of your education, and there are many factors that should be considered in terms of your schedule for each term. For starters, think about your educational goals, and identify which major or degree program you are working toward. Make sure you know and understand your degree options and requirements because these are important for both your academic progress and your athletic eligibility. Keep in mind that your academic eligibility is governed by your progress toward your degree. As you plan your course schedule, you need to be aware of matters such as prerequisites, which are courses that must be completed before you can elect other courses, the semesters when courses are offered and when they are not offered, and what times courses are typically offered and how they match up with your athletic commitments.

Another important aspect of course scheduling for student athletes has to do with whether you do better academically when you are in season or out of season. If you have a two-season sport, pay attention to the term in which your travel schedule is lighter or heavier. Don't assume you should take your more demanding classes out of season. Some student athletes do better with a more challenging schedule when they are in season because they are in a highly productive mode—more focused and most committed. Many students are also better time managers when they are the most busy and have to be most efficient. Other student athletes find they are just too tired to push themselves academically during their season. Figure out which type of student athlete best describes you and use that information strategically when you are selecting your classes. If you participate in a two-season sport, if at all possible, take your more demanding classes the term you travel least.

Balance is another important variable in putting together your course schedules. Make sure you have a good balance of courses with regard to the amount of reading, types of assignments, and types of exams. You do not want to be enrolled in four courses that all require extensive reading and lengthy papers. Nor do you want four courses in which grades are based exclusively on midterm and final exams because there is a fairly high likelihood that the exams will all be scheduled the same highly stressful weeks, and your entire course grade will be dependent on just those two exams. This requires research—finding the right balance for your schedule.

Speak with your academic advisor to help you balance your schedule. Your friends and teammates are good resources for information about courses too, but keep in mind that different students learn differently, and what one student finds difficult in a particular class, another may find easy.

One question students frequently ask is whether to register for one more class than necessary so you can drop a class if your class schedule turns out to be too challenging. The problem with this approach is that if you have actually overloaded your schedule from the beginning of the term, you will probably need to drop one course. If you have an appropriately balanced schedule, it is more likely that you will not need to drop any class.

Finalize your schedule as early as possible in each term. Students who add classes after the first week of the term almost never do as well as if they had been attending class from the first day. Make sure you know the course drop/add policies after the term starts. At some schools there will be more than one set of deadlines—one for the first few weeks and then one for later in the term. Be knowledgeable about these deadlines and procedures.

Each individual student's course scheduling decisions are unique. Work with your advisors to assess your best course schedule plan for each term. Each semester your academic and college success starts and ends with your classes. Use your resources to create your class schedule with the best information and advice available.

## 10. Learn to Think Critically

You know what it means to think. You've done a lot of hard work in high school that required you to think. You've heard about the importance of critical thinking a number of times in high school as your teachers tried to prepare you for the college experience. But what does it really mean to think critically?

An important premise of a college education is the expectation that a college-educated person will think insightfully and analytically about issues and can get to the root of the complex questions and challenges that face us personally and as a society. Unfortunately, too few students are actually required to think critically in high school. That includes those who score very well on standardized tests, write well-organized essays, and quickly complete advanced math assignments.

Critical thinking means that you are able to consider and analyze ideas, readings, debates, and discoveries in a comprehensive and thorough manner. It means that you can understand the nuances of an author's ideas and then can cogently challenge those ideas. It means that you can understand a point of view and then critique that point of view from multiple perspectives. It means you can hold several compelling but competing ideas and arguments in your mind at the same time and then examine the strengths and weaknesses of each. It means that you're impatient with two-sided debates because you realize that most issues have more than two sides and that most issues are far more complex than the discussion that any debate format will elicit. It means that you ask difficult questions of yourselves, others, and the physical world around you and that when you get reasonable answers to your questions, you ask a second and third set of questions that probe more broadly and more deeply.

The first college papers of some of the best prepared students are well-organized and well-written in terms of mechanics but are often lacking in substance. They just don't say much. In high school students were praised and rewarded for such papers, but in college they will be expected to do much more. These papers have good form but insufficient substance and analysis. These students too often haven't been challenged to think critically. By contrast, there are other students whose mechanical writing skills may be lacking, but in their lives they have had to ask difficult questions and to analyze and challenge the ideas and assumptions of others in deeper ways.

Both types of students (of course, these groupings are overly broad generalizations) will have considerable work to do in college. The good news is that they all have the ability to think critically. The problem is that, until college, few have been asked to do so.

The best approach to thinking critically is to ask questions to peel back layers of understandings. You should ask these questions about your own ideas, assumptions, and life, and you should also ask them about the ideas of others you meet through novels, articles, textbooks, and lectures. Go back again and again to probe and analyze. Accept your professors' feedback and perhaps initial lower grades with open arms because these experiences will challenge you to raise expectations for your work.

If you had already finished your learning and intellectual development, you wouldn't need to be in college. Learning to think critically will permit you to lead and excel in intellectual, civic, professional, and personal arenas, including your sport. It's one of the greatest gifts of a good college education.

## 11. Pay Attention to Academics Prior to and During Orientation ✐

Once you've been admitted to a college, you will start receiving information about your new school. You will receive this information during a busy time of your senior year of high school, but it is very important that you start paying close attention to the academic side of your equation as soon as you've decided on the college you'll be attending.

Start thinking about what you want to study in college by exploring what it is you want to read about, think about, talk about, and learn about. You will have many more choices of subjects to study than you had in high school so start looking through your college's website for information about the many different types of courses offered. Don't limit yourself to the options you know from your high school choices. That goes for college majors, as well. In college, you could very well choose to major in a subject you were not even familiar with in high school. The more time you give yourself to think about these questions, the better prepared you will be for student orientation, your first advising session, and selecting your first class schedule.

Orientation programs for first-year students are usually mandatory. They run anywhere from one to three days, sometimes in the months before you start college or, on some campuses, on the days right before your classes start. Find out how your college schedules and organizes orientation so you can plan accordingly. Many schools require new students to complete orientation "homework," or tasks to prepare for orientation ahead of time. Most orientation programs include placement testing for course selection, and many schools also provide online placement tests that students are required to take prior to attending orientation Since anything you are asked to do before and during orientation will affect decisions about which courses you take, it is obviously important to do it well.

During orientation you will receive information about various aspects of your college including campus resources, student life, and academic requirements, including information about majors and degree options. Most important, you need to understand how to select classes for your first term. If you don't know what you want to major in, definitely don't let that consume you at orientation. As an undeclared major, you will be joining a very large club of your peers, which is why many schools do not require students to declare majors until after their first or second year. However, if you think you know what you want to major in, and maybe even what you want to do "when you grow up" early in your college career, that's a bonus. In either case, keep an open mind to what interests and excites you along the way. You might change your mind.

This is also a good time to ask which majors require which pre-requisites and which courses might satisfy general requirements for a number of majors. Since many students change their majors while in college, find out which majors are more complicated to switch into later. Find out your school's policy for student athlete registration; some schools allow athletes to register early since their schedule time constraints are the result of university commitments. Ideally, orientation is a time to explore and consider your interests without any constraints, but be mindful of the reality that your best options may be impacted by your athletic commitments and/or obstacles for student athletes to major in certain areas or take certain courses. The sooner you know your realistic options and the "gate keeping" rules or obstacles that might exist at your school, the better you can plan accordingly to reach your academic goals.

College orientation programs are notorious for information overload. Your academic advisor will be there to help but you need to be your own best advocate right from the beginning. Find out about your athletic time commitments before you schedule your classes. Tell your advisor you want to be sure your course load is balanced in light of your athletic demands and commitments. Pay attention, ask questions, take notes, and follow up on anything you are unsure about. Orientation is your first real step into college; make it count.

# 4

# Discover Yourself and Your Identities: The Ball Is in Your Court

## 1. Model Good Behavior: Take Ownership of Your Identity as a Student Athlete

In high school, you heard the drill about the importance of representing your school, your team, and yourself with pride and honor. As you're learning with most things in college, this expectation will be even more important, more prevalent, and taken even more seriously as a college student athlete. Your good behavior is required at all times for several very important reasons.

Most student athletes on campus have name recognition and are physically recognizable or are easily identified by their letter jackets and other athletic attire. This means that other students, faculty, and staff, are more aware of how you conduct yourselves than they would be otherwise. For better or worse, you are noticed. Other students look up to you, want to get to know you, may be intrigued by your athletic accomplishments and the general mystique around college athletics. With this glory comes responsibility. You will be in a unique position to influence others and to make things happen for the greater good. You see this happen all the time with professional athletes and entertainers; they embrace their public roles and use them to promote their own passions and causes. As a visible and recognizable student athlete, you have the privilege, the responsibility, and the opportunity to make a difference in whatever good causes you decide to embrace.

College campuses have student organizations whose missions are to make the world a better place. The lists are often endless but almost always include goals such as putting an end to world hunger, fighting cancer and other diseases, improving literacy, taking care of the environment, providing assistance in the face of natural disasters, and many other worthwhile causes. Many athletic departments also have their own community service programs that provide opportunities for the athletes to give back to the local community that supports them.

As you know, the behavior of student athletes is regulated by several different entities, including the NCAA, your conference, your school, your athletic department, and your team. There are very specific regulations about what you can and cannot do and with whom and when. The penalty of not following these regulations can be disastrous and long term, resulting in the loss of your own eligibility at best and your school being placed on probation at worst. You will be given information about these regulations during your athletic orientation and on a regular basis after that. No student athlete wants to lose his or her eligibility or be responsible for putting the entire team on probation. Pay careful attention to these rules; the stakes are very high.

Of the many fans who may be paying attention to what you do and how you act, your youngest fans will be the most easily influenced by your good or bad behavior. Consider volunteering at a local elementary or middle school. When you have the platform, make sure you talk about the importance of being a good student in addition to being a good athlete. Any positive impact you can have on younger children, especially about issues such as educational opportunities, saying no to drugs or alcohol, and the importance of healthy eating and exercise, is worth its weight in gold.

Modeling good behavior will also be a catalyst for you to develop into a better person. While you might feel the need to relax at times, learning to do so in a safe and acceptable way can only help you stay out of trouble. If you are conscious of being in the public eye and representing your school and yourself well, chances are you will be quite successful at it, not to mention how proud you will make all of the important people in your life who have had a role in helping you become that successful college student athlete.

In addition to winning competitions, maybe even titles and championships, you have the chance to be an excellent role model and the best person you can be. Learn to use your student athlete status as a platform for positive change.

## 2. Identify Your Values and What's Most Important to You in Life

Who am I? What is the meaning of life? What am I doing here at this college? What does being an athlete mean to me? The weight of important existential questions of life can feel like a heavy burden, but they are essential for moving forward in life. Indeed, it is critical that you start the process of questioning during college.

College students love to write essays about their individual and group identities. They embrace these assignments because it requires them to look back on their experiences and reflect on their values, ideals, and identities. Invariably, they wonder how they can be graded on who they are, on their identities. Of course, it is the essay, and not the identity, that receives the grade. If you receive such an assignment, as many new students do, tell your story in the most thoughtful and reflective manner you can. This may be the beginning of your self-exploration.

In your first year of college, you will begin in earnest to shape and tell the story of what you find when you look deeply inside. Discover who you are now and who you could be. The deeper you allow yourself to probe and explore, the better able you will be to move forward with a strong foundation into adulthood. Don't be concerned if the answers aren't easily or immediately found. This is a process that should and does take time. At one time or another, you may question ideals you thought were entrenched in your value system, such as feelings about political or religious ideals or your athletic passion and commitment. Be comfortable exploring these thoughts. It does not mean you will change your mind or your feelings, but it is a way to optimize your personal growth and educational experience.

This introspection should take place in earnest during the college years, so be prepared to take ownership of it. You will find yourself with a whole new set of people surrounding you—new friends, new teammates, new classmates, new teachers, new advisors, and new coaches. With these new people and new surroundings, you have a unique opportunity to explore, experiment, establish, and assert who you are, what your identity is, and who you want to be in life. You have a golden opportunity to decide what you want to get out of your college education and experience, and what type of person you want to become while in college and for the rest of your life.

## 3. Find a Champion: Get a Mentor (Not a Booster)

We all benefit from good mentoring. As a college athlete you may have had the good fortune of finding a mentor or a mentor finding you in high school. You should give considerable thought to the idea of mentoring because you will do well to have mentors in college and throughout your life.

Mentors are people who take an interest in you; they represent a special mix of teacher, coach, advisor, and supporter for your professional, athletic, and academic (and, sometimes, personal) well-being. The best mentoring relationships are the products of special relationships that develop between the mentor and mentee. Mentors on occasion may have a personal stake in your professional success, but they most often are simply looking out for your best interests, without any self-interest involved. Mentors differ from parents, advisors, coaches, friends, teachers, and counselors, though each of those categories of people may at moments overlap and play roles similar to those of mentors. Mentors fall into a unique category all their own.

When a mentor gives you advice, he or she will first and foremost know what your interests and strengths are and will tailor the discussion very specifically to your individual needs, guiding you away from problem teachers and giving you tips on how to get into the most popular classes even when they are filled.

Mentors can give you the key to open locked doors. They can let you know when there is a great opportunity for an internship or when special speakers are coming to campus. They can strategize with you when you face obstacles. They can listen to you when you are confused. They can give you words of uplift and strength when you are feeling down, and they can help you figure out how to chart your course when you are ready to blaze new paths. Mentors truly care about the overall well-being and success of their mentees.

Colleges and athletic departments almost always have formal mentorship programs. They are a good start for learning about the mentoring relationship. They offer you well-meaning people who will take on the characteristics of a mentor in a formalistic role. At the same time, however, an assigned, formal mentor might not support and coach you with the passion and commitment of a mutually developed mentor relationship.

Take the initiative and responsibility to look for a mentor. The first step is to know that having a mentor is a good idea. The second step is to realize that a good mentoring relationship, like all good relationships, takes time to develop and requires continuing nurturance. Be patient and do not be demanding. The third step is to make sure you understand the NCAA rules about boosters and secondary agents (people who want to be your friend or mentor so they can connect you to an agent who will pay them for the connection). These specific and complex rules impact relationships that you have with any student or adult while you are a collegiate athlete. You must learn to distinguish between a mentor and a "groupie" (somebody who wants a relationship with you because of your athletic status). This is another area in which different rules apply to you than to the average student, and the stakes for you are high.

Try to develop relationships with people you respect and connect with at college. It's often as easy as following up on an instructor's comment of interest or praise about a paper you've written or a comment you've made in class. It can mean something as simple as visiting a professor's office hours to talk without having a very specific question or problem to present. Or, it could mean going to a professor or staff person on campus when you do indeed have a problem and taking the risk to trust someone with your personal story.

Good mentors will want time to get to know you, to determine whether they respect you as a person and as a professional. They will want to see the special spark of inner integrity and values that they admire. They will expect that you will be willing to share something about yourself. They will want to know that this will be a relationship that will continue over time. Successful mentoring relationships combine mutual respect, generosity, and giving, and will serve you well.

## 4. Develop Your Leadership Skills

A core goal of higher education is to develop an informed citizenry who will be active participants and leaders in a diverse democracy. You want to emerge from your college education as one of those active participants and leaders.

There are many different types of leaders and many different leadership opportunities. You should consider trying several of them to acquire experience and skills but also to see what best fits you. You have probably already had experience with the traditional model of leadership—a single head of a hierarchically arranged organization.

Living on your residence hall floor over the course of a year, you will be confronted with occasional roommate conflicts, arguments over loud music, inconsiderate and rude behavior, and perhaps even racial or religious insensitivities. Your floor will need a student who emerges as a leader, apart from the resident advisor, who will set the proper moral tone and create an environment in which people learn to talk through differences and disagreements.

In your classes, you can be an intellectual leader. You can do this by coming to class not only prepared (having completed the assignment) but also ready to ask probing questions and offer critical insights about the day's assignments. You can be a good listener and respond appropriately to other students' comments. You can attend faculty office hours. You can help organize study groups and support your fellow students who raise good issues or who come to you with questions.

In addition to hierarchical leadership, some people act as leaders through their ability to collaborate effectively with others. Working effectively in teams is a skill that most people require in all aspects of life, from the office to the community to home. Yet it is an exceedingly difficult skill and one that few people fully master. You are lucky to have such a head start as a member of an athletic team and community. Finding opportunities to develop this skill through study groups, group papers, lab projects, research projects, and planning events for student organizations will serve you well and give you valuable experience.

Another kind of leadership is that of the boundary crosser. Purposefully engage in meaningful ways with people from different backgrounds and settings that are new to you. You will begin to gain the ability and readiness to cross boundaries not only without fear but with anticipation for the rich learning and growth that emerge from those interactions and associations. Those who can do this well will be highly effective in managing social relations in their social life and in the workplace.

At some colleges you will have an opportunity to demonstrate leadership by serving as a student facilitator of course discussions. Student facilitators lead discussions in service-learning courses, intergroup dialogues, university 101–type courses, and other situations. Taking on this role requires responsibility, organizational skills, good discussion and listening skills, and the ability to assert oneself and intervene when necessary.

Finally, in addition to informal and formal opportunities to develop leadership skills, many colleges offer classes, workshops, and retreats on leadership. In these activities, you will do readings, review case studies, and learn what makes good leaders in all of the different styles where leadership exists and is necessary.

Students who participate in these activities tell us that they find them highly informative, empowering, and loads of fun. Most athletic departments also offer leadership training through life skills programs that are required by the NCAA. Create opportunities to develop your leadership skills now. They will stay with you throughout your life.

**Taylor King: "I'm not sure the big city suits me."**

*Taylor King grew up on a small dairy farm. Although he is a quiet, polite, and unassuming young man, he is well-known in his hometown. When you drive into Taylor's hometown of 232 people, a roadside sign greets you with the words "Welcome to the Home of the State Championship Wrestling Team." Taylor was the captain of the team.*

*As a farm boy and wrestler with his athletic talent, he didn't have the range of options that other athletes have to find the perfect fit in a college. He wanted a good coach, a good academic school, and a great scholarship. He did find one school that seemed to have everything he wanted with one exception: it was in the "big city."*

*Taylor's adjustment wasn't just about coming from a small town. He was also the first in his family to attend college. There was a lot to learn when he arrived at college. First, the school was bigger than his entire town. There was traffic, noise, lights, tall buildings, and lots of college offices and rules. Second, there were so many assertive, even aggressive, people.*

*Taylor was overwhelmed. He was going through the motions as he had been taught. He went to practice, worked out regularly, attended class, and did his homework. But, emotionally, Taylor was out of his league. He was homesick, lonely, sad, and lost. Academically, he was doing poorly.*

*Taylor had revered his high school wrestling coach. He revered him so much that he didn't want to confide his misery for fear the coach would be disappointed. He didn't want his college coach to be disappointed with him, either.*

*Taylor was sinking. He had met one person, his advisor, who seemed to understand his situation so Taylor decided to go to speak with her. It felt easy to talk with Carol. While she gave him lots of good advice, mostly he appreciated that she listened to him. And she understood that Taylor was an unhappy student athlete. Carol reviewed Taylor's course choices and pointed him to some small classes for the next term.*

*Taylor hadn't been sure he would return for his sophomore year, but he wanted to do the right thing and not disappoint everyone who* had put such faith in him and his future. So he came back. Still quiet and overwhelmed, he began to find that the small classes that Carol had suggested were very different from the large lecture classes. His teachers got to know him even though he was very quiet. The same was true with his peers.

It felt almost like a miracle that he once again had a close, small group of friends and also the respect of his teachers. It gave Taylor a renewed burst of self-esteem that he hadn't felt since high school. Instead of feeling like a fish out of water, Taylor started to feel more confident and relaxed. He smiled and laughed a lot more and started to enjoy life again. And he was doing much better in class.

By his junior year, Taylor had found himself and his place in college. Even though many on campus didn't follow the wrestling team, he had begun to realize his potential as a wrestling star. Academically, he had figured out how to be successful, and with his advisor and mentor, Carol, he identified good classes, caring teachers, and a major in history. He also realized the value of talking with his coaches about more than just wrestling.

By senior year, Taylor decided it was time to give back, and he was emotionally ready to do so. With the help of Carol and the athletic department, Taylor began a peer mentoring program for other students at the college who came from small towns or farms or who were first-generation college students. The satisfaction that he received from seeing first-year students get on track and find their place at college was as meaningful for this young man as all the wrestling awards he continued to accumulate and cherish.

## 5. Pursue Your Academic Dreams

Do you love to read history novels? Could you spend hours conceptualizing and then tinkering with the mechanics of a science project? Do you write poetry or do graphic arts in your free time? Are you consumed with the environmental crisis that global warming represents? Do you love to look at rock formations? Are you fascinated by the intersection of economics, international conflict, and ethnic hatred?

Dig deep into your life history and experience to come up with a list of subjects that you've found fascinating, troubling, exciting, and just plain worth your time to think about. Begin to identify what you really care about, and then find a way to pursue or at least explore these subject areas in college. Remember the discussion you had with your advisor at orientation about how to realistically assess your academic exploration, taking into consideration constraints that may exist due to curricular or athletic obstacles.

Many students imagine that there are significant constraints on their course selections. First, they are under the impression that they must immediately complete all of their distribution or general education requirements, or they take those courses because they are not sure what else to take. Second, they feel considerable pressure to take a prescribed set of courses that they believe are required to advance them toward particular majors and pre-professional degrees. Students interested in business, for instance, may feel pressured to major in economics, while students interested in law may feel pressured to major in political science. It is important to remember there are multiple paths to the same destination. At the undergraduate level, very few majors would preclude a student from entering a particular graduate program or being competitive for a specific career opportunity as long as other requisite courses are taken.

In truth, most students have a greater degree of flexibility to choose courses than they imagine when they first enter college. Yes, you do need to pay attention to general education or distribution requirements, and you should draft a plan of how you anticipate fulfilling those requirements during the first two years. But you have room for electives! Professional programs want applicants with a broad set of interests. In fact, interesting and unique credentials will strengthen your competitive edge in the graduate school and job market. Law schools would love to have a few more history or philosophy majors.

Think of your personal list of favorite subjects—your passions and interests—as another set of requirements that you fulfill during college, with equal standing to other requirements. You must effectively advocate for your personal set of requirements, your passions and interests, and negotiate the other general education, major, and pre-professional requirements to create a balance in your course schedule and in your life. Be a strong advocate for your own requirements because this negotiation will be one of the decisive factors in determining whether you feel satisfied with your college education.

Athletes are sometimes concerned that their practice or competition schedules interfere with selecting certain courses or majors. Most of the time coaches willingly support their athletes' academic goals and will accommodate conflicts with academic schedules when necessary. If you are concerned about this, talk to your coach and advocate for your academic opportunity.

Remember, this is *your* college education, and you only get one chance at it! You need to be true to yourself. Your school benefits from your athletic expertise. Your education is what you get in return. This is the time in your life to explore those topics that excite you and to pursue those dreams that drive your intellectual passions.

## 6. Hold Your Head High

For most college athletes, academic and athletic experiences are interwoven. You have both the privilege and the burden of your dual roles and identities. This is particularly true if you happen to be a high profile athlete on your campus. Other students cannot comprehend how it feels to be "known" by many students who don't really know you. Your public campus identity follows you into the classroom and the rest of your academic environment. As any college athlete can tell you, the exposure of a college athlete far exceeds the exposure of a high school athlete. It is important that you learn to manage this public persona and that you not allow it to get in the way of your academic business.

College students are sometimes reluctant to ask questions or engage in group discussions because they feel inadequate compared to other students in the class. Some student athletes will feel very comfortable in the academic arena while others may feel even more intimidated than most due to their visibility as athletes. Remember, many students struggle with the same concerns. Try to put a positive spin on this by considering that your classmates may have exactly the same questions or concerns, but they think that *you* are the one who is confident enough to express them. They may have had limited interaction with athletes of your caliber and may be impressed that you are academically focused and engaged in the discussion. They may be very interested to hear what you have to say precisely because you happen to be an athlete.

College athletes have the same general characteristics as the rest of the student population; some are very talkative and social, while others are quiet and shy. It is ironic that because college athletes are used to performing in front of large numbers of people, it is hard for many non-athletes to imagine them as shy individuals.

College athletes, however, have yet another challenge that non-athletes never have to face: going to class and walking around campus after the big win. To be congratulated, high-fived, and cheered on for the big win or a great personal performance is, of course, gratifying. But it can also take a toll on an individual to have to be "on" and be responsive to people all around campus. It can also make it hard for student athletes in the classroom where they want to be like everyone else and have the privilege of learning but are often only recognized for being athletes.

It can be even more difficult for student athletes on campus after the big loss or after a poor individual or team performance. Sometimes they are subjected to bad behavior on the part of some fans who don't respect the boundaries that should exist for student athletes on campus and in the classroom. It requires a high level of maturity and resilience to hold your head high in those circumstances. Remember, the game is never won or lost by one person's performance. The score is the total of the performance of the entire team, including the coaches.

You have a responsibility to yourself to take full advantage of your academic opportunity. Whether you happen to be on the shy side, are uneasy that you are more visible than other students, or are reeling from a big win or a big loss, you must not compromise your academic goals and mission.

## 7. Be an Ideal Roommate

You'll be happiest if you start with positive yet modest expectations for your relationship with your roommate. You may hope for a perfect match, but you'll be more realistic if you anticipate that you'll have a reasonably respectful and civil relationship. Remember, you will spend eight to ten months in a small room or suite, almost entirely filled with beds, desks, and dressers, together with a person (or persons) you may have just met. Chances are you will have a perfectly good relationship, but don't count on a perfect one. At most colleges, teammates room together, and the housing assignments are made by a staff member involved in recruiting who can make good matches because he or she knows the incoming students.

Students may have pre-conceived ideas about their college roommates. You may have heard stories or watched TV shows or movies where roommates become best friends and confidants for the rest of their lives. You may be thinking that you'll have similar tastes in friends and in room decoration and will share values about neatness and cleanliness. Your hope is that you'll share fears, celebrate successes, stay up late at night talking, and eat popcorn while watching favorite movies and playing video games. If you live with a teammate, you may believe that you will share the special bond of understanding the full student athlete experience and that you will support each other along the way.

Although this type of relationship could develop, the opposite scenario may also occur. You and your roommate may not agree about how you want to share your small living space. If you room with a teammate, you may be too competitive athletically to feel comfortable living together. But deeper fears about a roommate, things like whether he or she will steal your money or clothes, or lock you out of the room, or is involved in some illegal activity, are so unlikely that you should not waste any time worrying about it. The actual experience of most students is a modestly positive one.

You and your roommate are likely to get along just fine, although there may be some bumps in the road. You probably won't be each other's closest friend in the world, but you will share the experiences of one of your most memorable years. You will be able to negotiate most issues, such as differences about noise levels when one is sleeping, study time, and how to divide up the refrigerator. You may even end up liking and befriending some of your roommate's good friends.

It is critical that you approach your relationship with your roommate with respect, sensitivity, and civility. You have to learn to listen to his or her point of view, speak up for yourself and your views, speak openly and honestly, negotiate differences directly, and talk through any problems or disagreements.

Contact your roommate as soon as you learn who it is. If you don't know each other, you will still have a lot in common as teammates. Don't rush to set up or decorate your room the day you move in without waiting to talk with your new roommate. Expect that he or she will have some different lifestyle habits and some different values from you. He may stay up late to study, while you go to bed early to wake up for eight o'clock classes. She may have siblings and may have shared a room at home, while you have no siblings and have always had your own room. Your roommate will likely be different in some social identity, be it race, religion, class, ethnicity, or sexual orientation. Don't even think about the idea of rejecting a roommate because he or she comes from a different background. Be open to those differences, learn from them, and celebrate them.

As a first-term student, it's not a good idea to room with your best friend. Yes, it can work in some cases, but more often best friends stay best friends when they don't live together. The best advice is to follow that age old golden rule: treat your roommate with the same respect and consideration you want and expect in return. Chances are you will get along just fine!

## 8. Avoid People Who Want to Use You ⚊⚊

High school was probably a wonderful experience for you with great memories from that time of your life. Now, however, it's time to move on with the rest of your life. Still, you want to be able to hold onto the good relationships you had with your closest friends and other acquaintances.

Your first priority must be to establish your independence and build new friendships in college. To do this and to also keep good relationships with your best high school friends requires a conscious effort on your part. Your close high school friends, the ones you will keep in touch with, will want to hear about your college life, your athletic accomplishments, and your new friends. With your new friends and teammates, you will have the bond of sharing new experiences and discoveries together. As the lyrics to a traditional Girl Scouts song aptly describe: "Make new friends but keep the old; one is silver and the other gold." That motto should work for you, too, while you are in college.

How will you choose your friends? Be sure to surround yourself with good people. Choose friends you can trust and who will care about your well-being. Look at their values and judgments. Be sure you respect them. Be open to interacting with and learning from all different kinds of people. And, when you choose your closest friends, be selective because you may be establishing life-long friendships with the people you meet in college.

Electronic communication and social media have changed the nature of "friendships." Student athletes need to be very careful about the content and endless life cycle of what is posted on the Internet and sent via email. Learn to manage your college email account wisely. Since student athletes' names are public and listed in the college's online directory, athletes often receive email from people they don't know. Higher-profile athletes can receive hundreds of unwanted emails a day. Learn the tricks to best organize your accounts so you can easily find the emails you need and want. Do not waste your time or risk compromising your eligibility by responding to emails from strangers.

Additionally, most students have phones with cameras so actions that seem to be happening between friends or in the privacy of friends can quickly become public on the Internet. Another hazard of social media is that it affords less protection against those with ulterior motives for befriending student athletes. This places even more responsibility on student athletes to "vet" people who contact them electronically.

Caution aside, developing friendships is a two-sided street. It requires that you be a friendly person yourself. Be prepared to open yourself up to your close friends and make sure they know they can open up to you. Friends should be there for you when you need them, but you need to be there for them, too, even at inconvenient times.

Your teammates, of course, will be among your closest friends, but do not exclude others from becoming part of your trusted inner circle just because they are not athletes or teammates. Unfortunately, you also must be aware of people who try to befriend you simply because you are an athlete. You may have already been exposed to this kind of behavior in high school, but this is often a much bigger problem in college. If you have concerns about someone's intentions, focus on the non-athlete aspects of your friendship to see if that person still wants to hang out with you and be your friend.

If you surround yourself with good people, they will give you good advice. They will steer you in positive directions. They will set high expectations for your behavior and values. They will not get you into dangerous situations or ask you to do things you know to be wrong. You will become a better person for those friendships, as will your friends.

CHAPTER 5

# Explore the Campus and Expand Your Horizons: From the Locker Room to the Press Conference

## 1. Learn Outside the Classroom

Some of the most important lessons you will learn in college will take place outside the classroom. You can learn from every individual you encounter and every activity you participate in, no matter where or when those interactions take place, as long as you make a point of reflecting on those encounters and experiences. College is an environment of intentional learning. Begin to think of yourself as an intentional learner. Maximize your opportunities for learning as deeply and as broadly as possible from all your college-related experiences, including being a college athlete.

You should consider a variety of categories of learning outside the classroom. Consider first what may seem to be the easiest and most natural — just hanging out with friends. At college, you have a chance to broaden your scope of friends. If you step outside your room, you are likely to meet individuals who come from a much wider variety of racial, ethnic, religious, class, and sexual orientation backgrounds than you have previously been exposed to or been friendly with. Get to know these people. Make friends with them. In time, open up yourself to them about your background and learn about theirs.

Get involved. There will be opportunities within your athletic department to serve on committees and participate on various projects. Even though you are busy, you can still join campus clubs or organizations. Get involved in your residence hall, student government, or ethnic or religious group on campus. You might be surprised to learn how busy many other students are, too. Volunteer for a community service project, take on an internship, or find a job if your athletic scholarship permits you to earn money. All of these activities will give you insight into how organizations and people within organizations work in different sectors of society. Are the organizations highly structured or unstructured, hierarchical or authority sharing? Do people involved work competitively or collaboratively, do they do things together outside of work, or does everyone go their own way immediately after a meeting or the job is done?

Attend all sorts of campus events, including those that are social, educational, and cultural. Go to sporting events. Attend an opera, a chamber orchestra concert, a comedian's performance, or a musical production. Go to a debate about global warming, a speech on race relations, a talk about the human genome, a workshop on getting along with your roommate, a documentary about endangered species. Go by yourself, with a friend, with a large group from your residence hall, or with your teammates. You will be exposed to a wide range of life from many different vantage points. Enjoy yourself as you learn about the world around you.

Get involved in campus and community organizations. Run for an office in student government. Take a position in a departmental club. Train to become a student facilitator for an intergroup dialogue class. Be a site leader one day a week for the local food kitchen. Let a faculty member or dean know that you'd like to be a student representative on a faculty or school committee. Attend leadership workshops or retreats. You will learn about different kinds of people and leadership styles, where your strengths lie, and how you like to participate in organizations. There is time to do these things too—you are not only a student and an athlete.

College is an all-day, every day learning experience. Take advantage of the immense learning opportunities available both inside and outside of the classroom.

## 2. Embrace Your Academic and Scholarly Community

College connotes different things to different people. We hope you'll be one of those students who thinks of college as a community—or, more specifically, a scholarly community—in which you get to spend four or five years of your life with a group of people who are deeply engaged with ideas, exploration, questioning, discovery, analysis, and problem solving. To do so will most definitely put you in the right mindset for a successful college experience.

Consider for a moment some other ideas about college. For some students, college is like an extended summer camp where the primary goal is to make great friends, party, and have as much fun as possible while you pick up a degree along the way. For others, it is a professional training ground where you are preparing for a lucrative career, maybe even as a professional or Olympic athlete. Still others think of it as a place of competition and endless judgment, with tests and exams and grades.

Why should you approach your college experience as a scholarly community? Let's take the community aspect first. It's important to surround yourself with good people. As you grow and develop personally, socially, and intellectually, it's so much healthier to do so in a supportive environment of thinking, caring people. It is in this sense of community that college is far more than a set of requirements or courses or credits to complete. You have the unique opportunity to think, study, and grow surrounded by and engaged with other bright, thinking people.

In terms of the scholarly aspect of college, it's important that you begin to self-identify as both a young scholar and a college athlete. This piece of advice is not intended to pigeonhole you or limit you socially—in fact, it will probably do just the opposite. It will prevent you from becoming overly parochial by allowing you to grow and expand exponentially.

Personal and social growth is, of course, essential, but what makes college unique is the attention to analytic thinking, books, lectures, discussions, critical insights, discoveries, and information. You have the opportunity to be a part of and contribute to a collection of people, faculty and students alike, who are focused on learning, exploring, and thinking deeply about all sorts of issues, topics, and inquiries.

Once you've received your notice of admission to college, it's actually very easy to become a part of the scholarly community. The hardest part is to make a shift in your mindset. Instead of thinking of coursework as a series of assignments, tests, and homework, you need to think of it as a great opportunity for learning. Instead of thinking of your teachers as people who judge you and have control of grading, imagine them as mentors, fellow thinkers, senior colleagues, and scholarly friends and allies. Look at bulletin boards or the school newspaper and attend the daily guest lectures and talks on campus. Go to theater productions, art exhibits, and classical concerts. Read national and global newspapers. Peruse scientific and popular magazines that address intellectual issues. Visit faculty in their offices. Go to receptions, book signings, and poetry readings. During your off season commit to trying new activities. Hang out with your friends from your classes or in your residence hall late at night and talk about an exciting or controversial idea from your class that day.

## 3. Seek Opportunities Outside of Athletics

It is rare that a college athlete has not been heavily involved in athletics through most of his or her youth. To be selected as a college-level athlete requires skill and expertise that often takes years to develop. You may have found that your development as an athlete did not leave you with too much time for other activities. Fellow athletes are the people with whom you probably spent the most time and shared the most in common. Your current social network and circle of friends most likely is still predominantly made up of athletes since being an athlete is an integral aspect of who you are. Think about college as a way to expand your horizons by casting a wide net around the activities you select and the people you'd like to get to know.

In college, you will have easy access to people all around you who will be different from you in any number of ways. There will be first-generation college students. There will be students from big cities, small towns, other states, and other countries; students from big families and from small families; students who are immigrants and students who can trace their families to the Mayflower. There will be students with interests, skills, and experiences in as many different subjects as your school has majors. You may find that you have more in common with someone who has a different life experience.

An easy way to start exploring new activities and meeting new people is by getting to know your classmates, the students in your residence halls, and your teammates. Chances are you have not spent too much time talking with your teammates about much other than your common athletic experiences and goals. You might be surprised by what you can learn about each other.

Another easy way to get to know others is to join study groups with non-athletes and to take advantage of academic resources open to all students on your campus. You may be required to attend study table or work with tutors through your athletic department academic support program. Attending additional study groups and making use of campuswide academic support services will enhance the rest of your study regimen, in addition to providing you with the extra bonus of interpersonal growth and development.

Make the time to get involved in activities outside of athletics. Even if you have very limited time, you can occasionally choose activities that expose you to life on your campus outside of your athletic universe. For some students, spending all their time with other athletes is simply a matter of having limited time; for others, exploring the world beyond their athletic comfort zone may be a real social and emotional stretch. While it is true that your athletic involvement provides you with endless meaningful opportunities, experiences, and relationships, you owe it to yourself to explore the other great opportunities and experiences that your college and the surrounding community have in store for you.

**Lauren Mason: "It's 'team' on the court, but strangers off the court."**

*Lauren loved the unity of her basketball team. Everyone was all about the "team." And it was paying off. The basketball team was off to its best start in the last five years.*

*One of the things Lauren loved about her college team was the coach's complete commitment to the team-first concept over individual accomplishments. Everyone on the team had been a star in high school, and they all knew about personal heroics, stats, and being the center of attention. Unfortunately, most of the players on* the team also knew about losing games, about team dissension, jealousy, and distrust.

This year's team was the most diverse Lauren had ever played on. There were teammates from the wealthy suburbs, big cities, rural areas, prep schools, and poor urban areas. Not only did it not seem to matter, but in some ways the diversity of each player seemed to contribute to the overall betterment of the team's play. Each one came from different leagues with different styles of play and different strengths but with a singular purpose of winning.

And, yet, Lauren could not get over the fact that this same "team" on the court invariably went in very different and separate paths off the court. The white teammates went to parties populated mostly by white women and men. The African-American teammates hung out with African-American friends and went to parties and campus events with those same friends.

Lauren thought it odd that no one talked about this. The racial separation off the court didn't cause the kind of surprise and upset to others that it did for Lauren. On the one hand, Lauren thought, how could it be that we're such a unified team on the court but live such separate social lives off the basketball court? On the other hand, Lauren was not naïve, and she realized that this seemed to be the way things typically played out on most other teams at her college and at most colleges everywhere.

Lauren wasn't the kind of person to rock the boat, but she thought that the off-the-court separation could make the team unsteady in its play as the year wore on. So rather than make a public statement but still wanting to do something, Lauren took it as *a personal mission to start mixing it up with her white teammates. At first, she just starting sitting at the lunch table with some of the white women. Then she persuaded one of her African-American teammates to go with her to one of the white parties. It wasn't the greatest time, and there were some strange looks, but it went okay.*

*Becky, the starting point guard who was white, took note of what Lauren had initiated and decided to follow her lead. Becky had never thought much about race issues, but she was observant enough to see that the campus was about 90 percent white and that most white students never attempted to leave their racial comfort zone and interact and make friends with the African-American students and other non-white students. Becky invited the other African-American guards to go to the movies with her one evening. That was a first. It broke the ice.*

*It turned out to be a very successful season. Although the team didn't win the league championship, it did go to the national playoffs for the first time in years and made it through the first two rounds. Off the court, no one ever became best friends across the racial divisions, but Lauren felt that she and others had made some inroads. On the court there was no question that they clearly knew and valued what the word "team" meant and, for many on her team, they had taken the first steps out of their previously separate lives. They had begun to learn what the concept of "team" might mean off the court, in their daily lives, in their communities, and in the rich diversity of America's democratic society.*

## 4. Take Safe Academic Risks

College is a time to step out and find your true personal, academic, and professional interests. It's a time for safe and thoughtful reflection, experimentation, and affirmation.

Taking risks means moving out of your comfort zone. It means expanding your intellectual horizons and exploring the world of opportunities that lie before you.

When you arrive at college, don't just get busy fulfilling requirements—take some courses you like. Did you always want to know more about paintings in the art museum? Study art history. Have you wanted to feel like you can understand the business section of the newspaper? Take an economics course. Was your favorite school assignment one where you collected different kinds of leaves in second grade? Then take a biology class or environmental studies or geology—all of those fields might bring you back to an original intellectual passion.

Like it or not, too much of your time and attention will likely be spent worrying about what grades you will receive in your classes. Your purpose at college is to learn. Yet our education system, to a deleterious extent, has tried to equate grades with learning. They're not the same.

Too many students look at the grade on a paper or test and then ignore the instructor's extensive comments. Students often ask whether an assignment will be on the test, thinking there is no intrinsic value in the course assignments but only how they will be factored into grades. Faculty-student conversations and office hours are too often focused on test preparation and grade appeals/complaints rather than opportunities for learning and participation in the scholarly community.

One way to expand your horizon academically is to take classes that really stretch your comfort zone. Taking a pass/fail class is a great way to explore new ideas and fields in college. A pass/fail course allows you to focus on what you learn in a course without the pressure and interference of a grade. It also provides you with an opportunity to safely experiment in your course selection without having to be overly concerned about getting a lower grade by taking a course that you think will be particularly challenging.

The pass/fail option allows you to take safe risks in your course selection. A non-science major who is interested in chemistry but worries that she might get a low grade competing with pre-med students can take the course pass/fail and just drop all the worries. A student studying Spanish for his or her second language requirement might want to take a semester of Chinese but worries about ruining an otherwise high grade point average. Taking the class pass/fail may be just the answer.

Find out what other options your school has to promote this type of learning and academic exploration. Your school may have opportunities for doing research projects for credit or for taking an independent study with a professor you have taken a course with and with whom you want to explore in-depth a topic not being offered as a regular college course. Consider all of these options and, of course, be sure to find out the implications of pass/fail or other grading on your athletic eligibility.

Learning for learning's sake, in ways that allow for different pathways to knowledge and are without the mediating presence of a grade, are likely to be liberating educational experiences. You will quickly appreciate what people mean when they speak of the love of learning.

## 5. Learn Another Language

Many U.S. citizens wonder why there is even a need for second language instruction. After all, English is spoken throughout the United States and in many parts of the world. One need only think about the global economics of sports and the global reach of athletic competition to understand why learning a second language in today's world is so important.

The world grows smaller and more interconnected each day. For you, as today's college student and tomorrow's professional, the nations of the globe will seem much more like the proverbial global village than anyone can begin to imagine now. Further, the multilingual global village increasingly resides not just in foreign countries but within the U.S. borders as well.

The speed of travel, the instant communication of the global Internet, the rapid expansion of global business networks, and the natural resources that know no boundaries and that we increasingly share across the globe will lead us to have much more frequent and consistent contact with people everywhere. Literature, movies, politics, business, and trade cross our borders every day whether or not we choose to acknowledge the massive interdependence of the peoples throughout the world.

It has always been the case, and it is no different today, that we know we can understand and communicate better across cultures if we know the language of different cultures. Language in translation is considerably different and less rich than the original. The precise meanings, the cultural understandings, and the delicate nuances of language cannot be adequately captured in translation.

Much of the world already speaks more than one language. As you increasingly think of yourself as a global citizen as well as a citizen of a particular nation, you will need to speak a second language to keep up. Even the United States itself is increasingly becoming a bilingual or even multilingual nation, and to move comfortably across the business, athletic, and cultural sectors within this society, you should be conversant in more than one language.

Can you imagine traveling abroad and speaking that country's language? Or applying for a job or promotion for which you will have a competitive edge because you speak the language and understand the culture of your business partners and clients? How would it feel to be so immersed culturally that you could watch a movie, listen to music, perhaps with lyrics, or read an online newspaper in the language you studied? These are the kinds of experiences and activities that will help make you a global citizen of the world.

When you receive your college degree, you will want to think of yourself as an educated individual. Learning a second language will give you even more reason to make that claim.

# 6. Explore Religion and Spirituality

In a society so focused on wealth and material goods, many students today are looking for something more meaningful in their lives. Some are looking for the comfort, faith, and solace of a god or religion to help them make sense of the world, while others are searching for answers in spirituality or a spiritual community.

You may identify closely with a particular religion when you arrive at college, or you may be less closely affiliated with an organized religion but still want to find deeper meaning and commitments in your life. This interest in organized religion or a search for spirituality is increasingly true of students who are attending college today.

Many campuses have a variety of religious-affiliated campus organizations. These organizations seek to provide a place on campus to explore religion or spirituality. They are student-centered and usually offer both religious and social activities to encourage your involvement and pursuit of religion while in college with a group of peers from the same faith.

Some students either object to organized religions or have found that they do not provide the spiritual foundation and grounding they are seeking. These students may discover what they are looking for in books, nature, friendships, and meaningful connections with like-minded people who are searching for something deeper in life.

Some students try to convert other students to join a different religion or to follow a particular religious or spiritual path they have chosen for themselves. Students do not appreciate being proselytized on college campuses by their fellow students. Over the years, some groups have periodically misrepresented their mission and preyed on college students, attempting to recruit impressionable college students to join cults. Be forewarned about groups that misrepresent their intentions. Students seeking social networks are most vulnerable to accepting invitations from strangers that may have hidden agendas.

These searches for faith, religion, spirituality, and meaning in life are likely to be of great importance to you, just as they have been to generations of humans seeking to understand the mysteries and the commonplace of our lives. Use the many resources available on campus and surrounding your campus. Consult with many peers and elders, but don't just follow what other folks, both the well meaning and the untrustworthy, tell you to do or believe. Find your own answers and path. Be smart and thoughtful about this and take your time on this important journey.

## 7. Make the Most of Your Travel Opportunities

College student athletes have substantial travel opportunities thanks to athletic competitions that require travel to campuses across the country. Many teams travel to places with better climates to train. A number of sports teams participate in championship games, post-season games, and tournaments. All of these provide you with important learning opportunities in terms of being exposed to different places, people, and cultures.

Exposure to different parts of this country or the world can also prepare you for a professional career that requires you to be culturally aware and sensitive to the perspectives and experiences of people living in different parts of the globe. Even during quick trips, take note of the differences from your hometown or college town.

As a college athlete, you may already be thinking "I can't do this" when you think about studying and traveling abroad. Study abroad is the opportunity to study and live in another country, immersed in that country's culture, including classes. Such opportunities can range from several weeks to a full year. Yes, there are a number of factors that make it more complicated for college athletes to participate in study abroad programs, but it is not impossible. The opportunity for you to study abroad will depend on a variety of factors, including your competition schedule, your training needs, the type of scholarship and/or financial aid you are receiving, and the implications for eligibility. Such opportunities are a very important part of the college experience, and you should look into whether it will be possible at some point for you to participate in a study abroad program. The world has become a much smaller place than it has ever been before, and your generation has grown up with the recognition that we live in an interdependent, global society. You should see and experience the global society first-hand.

There are increasing numbers of short-term and innovative programs that include service learning, internships, research projects, or educational initiatives that may be more feasible options for athletes. If you'd like to explore whether you might be able to study abroad, check first with your coach, compliance officer, and scholarship expert. If you can find a program sponsored by your college, you may be able to have your scholarship and/or financial aid applied to that program.

If you get a thumbs up, move on to speak with your academic advisor about how particular programs fit with your degree requirements.

If you are lucky enough to compete out of the country, make the most of the opportunity to be exposed to a different way of life. You will encounter new cultures, values, and foods as well as different languages, news reports, economic systems, and governmental structures. You will find that people in other countries don't always view your way of life as the centerpiece of how they see and experience the world.

If you are not able to study abroad during college, don't be discouraged. Consider programs available to new post-college graduates that provide similar opportunities but are based on service or employment. Most important, wherever and whenever you travel, learn, engage, immerse yourself, and take in all you can to make the most of the experience.

**CHAPTER**

# Make a Difference in the World: Step Up to the Plate

## 1. Take Responsibility for the World Around You

You bring a new set of eyes to the world around you. As a college student, you have the ability to see problems and opportunities that older people may not see so clearly. Each generation has the chance—even the responsibility—to learn from the past and present and to make changes to improve and sustain society for the future. This isn't a frivolous responsibility; it is one you should accept with respect, courage, and commitment.

College is a time when you get to think a lot about yourself—your development, growth, personal ambitions, relationships, and academic and athletic success. It is actually quite important that you take the time necessary to think hard about the kind of person you want to be as an adult.

At the same time, it's just as important that you begin to see yourself as someone who can and should make a significant impact on the world around you. Just as there is a value in looking after your own well-being, as citizens of our communities, cities, nations, and world, we also need to look after the well-being of those around us.

There is, in fact, a long tradition in the United States and elsewhere of college students asking hard questions of college and political leaders about societal conditions. Those questions have often been linked to student activism and taking a stand for moral principles.

There are a number of ways to think about this social responsibility. First, taking responsibility for others is a sign of moving from childhood, when you are the responsibility *of* others, to adulthood, when you are responsible *for* others. Second, taking responsibility for other people and for societal issues is a positive sign of empowerment, indicating that you consider yourself a full-fledged member of society and that you feel you have the motivation and power to actually contribute to the well-being of others and to create change in society. Third, it demonstrates that you have enough confidence in yourself to give some of yourself to others.

How might you take responsibility for the world around you? There are many approaches to do so, and you should find the ways that best fit your personality. One way to do this is through your personal relationships—that is, how you relate to acquaintances, friends, and even strangers. Do you interrupt racist, anti-Semitic jokes, or dumb jock jokes? Do you behave respectfully toward the man or woman with whom you develop a romantic relationship? Do you speak openly and honestly about people around you, whether they are present or not?

Others may find that they can give back to society most constructively through community service and volunteer work, by tutoring in a school, by volunteering in a hospital, or by serving in an organization and on its committees. Still others decide to run for political office, to vote in elections, to write letters to the editor, or to contest the decisions of college administrators or political leaders. As high-profile students on college campuses, and often in their years beyond college, athletes have a unique opportunity to model behavior that embraces these concepts.

Decide what approach best fits who you are. This process may take some time. Look at the world around you, and work to make it a better place than when you entered it.

## 2. Withhold Assumptions about People

You walk onto campus and you see someone looking at you. You've never met this person, but you can tell that he's sizing you up. He's drawing a mental picture of who you are, putting you into a small and limiting box. You are likely getting more upset by the minute, guessing he's making assumptions about you because you're an athlete.

No one would question that he is drawing a distorted, stereotypical picture of you. At the same time, the truth is that almost all of us do the same kind of sizing up of other people around us, making judgments and drawing on stereotypical images of all kinds of unique individuals around us.

So what's the problem? The problem is that when others do this to us or we do the same to others around us, we lose sight of the very special, unique characteristics that each of us prides ourselves on as individuals. We erase the individuality and soul of each person around us. As is usually the case, we miss out on opportunities to meet all kinds of amazing people.

Especially for the vast majority of college students, who come from homogeneous backgrounds, the stereotyping and dismissal of people based on physical characteristics represents a tremendous opportunity lost. A woman with blond hair—haven't we been taught throughout our lives a negative, stereotypical image about that person's intelligence? A man with an earring—is that truly supposed to give us clear insight into that person's personality and values? A southern accent in a northern state or vice versa—do any of us really believe that we can learn anything substantive about someone's personality from an accent?

Yet, so many college students are inclined to go ahead and forge friendships with or avoid people according to these grand assumptions based on so little (mis)information. Some of us will set high or low expectations of people based on what region of the country they come from. "Oh, you're from New York?" Or, "You're an athlete." "Well, I've got you all figured out. I know what you're all about." Surely, if we paused for just an instant, all of us would know that this one person cannot possibly be exactly like the other millions of people in New York City or that all college student athletes are the same.

The sad part is that many other students may be judging you in the same way. How wrong and simplistic can they be! Yet all these college students are supposed to be so smart! Be smarter than they are. Try this: Every time you meet a new person at college, withhold your assumptions about him or her. Try to actually meet and get to know the person behind the handbag, the t-shirt, the skin color, the city they come from, the accent, or the weight and height. Get to know each person's individual values, history, aspirations, humor, and friends. Find out about others just as you'd hope they would want to learn about you.

This approach not only will give you a chance to make real, lasting friendships with people from all backgrounds but along the way will help you to learn to like yourself a lot more as you give yourself and others a chance to grow beyond the little boxes into which we sort ourselves.

## 3. Be a Boundary-Crosser

Leaders of your generation will be boundary-crossers. You should learn to be one as part of your college education. Boundary-crossers can move easily across groups and categories of people. They have the attitude, skills, and mindset that allow them to transcend the social barriers that most people don't dare cross. Boundary-crossers are respectful of other people and are interested in their commonalities and differences. They are good listeners but are just as willing and ready to fully engage. They are open and honest. Boundary-crossers see connections and opportunities for collaboration. They are expert at linking people together locally, nationally, and globally. They don't see walls, they see pathways.

Boundary-crossers are comfortable with people, ideas, and organizations. They have a natural curiosity about all kinds of subject matter, and they find people's lives and stories intriguing. They are problem solvers, connectors, and bridge-builders. They don't need to be at the top of the hierarchy, but we'd all be a lot better off if more of them were. They can move easily across the different ranks of personnel within an organization.

As a college student, you can both learn and practice the skills of boundary-crossers. As an athlete and member of a team, you have a built-in opportunity to practice these skills with your teammates, people with whom you already share a safe level of trust. By intentionally working to expand your comfort zone, you will begin to gain a level of ease being with people from different social backgrounds. By getting to know the persons behind particular viewpoints, you will appreciate how even well-educated, well-meaning, and very likeable people can differ dramatically on politics and issues of intellectual interest. By taking a broad array of courses across various disciplines, you will gain an understanding about why and how different people can be so intrigued by and even passionate about topics that you hadn't even heard of.

In college you will find the same walls set up to divide people and organizations that exist in society at-large. Students will divide themselves up by their social identity groups. Those students with different political views from their neighbors won't associate with each other except to shout their views louder than the next person.

You can be different. You can bring people and organizations together. You can be friends with individuals from different political parties as easily as you can be friends with people who have different majors. You can engage your peers regarding contentious issues but still leave the discussion with respect for one another. You can find common ground and opportunity in difference.

In becoming a boundary-crosser, you will find that your learning increases exponentially by moving across and between boundaries. You will find that your friendships are as deep as they are wide. You will learn to see value and opportunity in almost every person, idea, issue, and organization you encounter. You will be prepared to take on leadership roles in your family and community. In civic life, in business, and throughout your professional life, you will be a much sought-after person. You will experience the world more positively, and you will make the world a more positive place in which to live.

## 4. Find Your Voice and Take a Stand

Kids have opinions from a very young age, and they know how to express themselves. They're quick to let you know what they're thinking. Over the next 18 years, however, through parenting, schooling, and other socializing institutions, children and especially teenagers are taught not to have their own opinions. They're told it's rude to disagree with an adult. Their high school writing teachers tell them not to invoke a personal view into papers (unless asked) or use the first-person pronoun *I*.

Along comes college, and suddenly professors are asking you for your opinion and expecting you to have one! "How does your personal experience inform the theory of this author?" your professor will ask. You may at times be asked to write in the first person. You might be challenged to rediscover the *I* in your vocabulary and thought processes.

While this concept sounds reasonable as an aspect of college student development, it becomes more complicated for student athletes. The nature of the athlete-coach relationship requires a certain level of obedience. Coaches consider this an aspect of the coachability of an individual. Generally speaking, athletes tend to concede more than the typical non-athlete because they are entrenched in the dynamics of a subordinate relationship with their coaches. So, how do you blend the appropriate level of obedience required as a college athlete with the appropriate level of independence and thought-provoking challenge expected of you in other aspects of your college life? As with most things in life, you must learn to find the balance.

You will be able to assess your coach's communication and coaching style early on. It may be acceptable for you to question or challenge your coach in a conversation between the two of you, but it will most likely not be acceptable for you to challenge your coach in a team meeting. Conversely, your professors will continuously encourage you to think independently, to question, and to challenge what you read, learn, and hear in college.

As you walk across the college campus, students might confront you about your views on the upcoming election—whom are you voting for, and why? They might want to know your opinion about foreign affairs. They will ask you to join a demonstration for or against a civil rights issue. You might be engaged in a conversation about a conservative or liberal speaker and be expected to know who the speaker is and whether or not you support his or her view.

You will be asked about religion, about organized religious institutions, and more generally about faith and spirituality. You will be questioned about the ethnic joke or gender joke you make at someone's expense. It may have sounded funny and harmless at the high school lunch table, but in college, you may be challenged to consider and defend the sensibility of that humor.

There will be campus issues you'll be expected to think about, too. Is tuition too high? Should there be a student-run bookstore? Do you support a "safe walk" program on campus? Should professors give final exams before the last day of class? What hours should be set for quiet time on your residence hall floor? Should college athletes be paid? Should they be allowed to register before everybody else because of their practice schedules?

These questions may seem overwhelming and yet very exciting at the same time. What if you don't know enough to have an informed opinion? How do you learn about these things? What if you don't care or never cared before? What if you care really deeply and want to become a leader of one of these groups?

Everyone in society is trying to tell us what we should believe. There are loads of sound-bite answers to complex questions in society that truly require clear, critical, and complex answers. As a college-educated person, you will want to understand the complexities of issues and to arrive at answers that go beyond traditional, simplistic solutions. The starting point is to realize that your opinion matters and that society needs you to have that opinion. Don't let others form your views for you. Your educated view and voice matter.

### Ben Whitaker: "The sex talk"

*Ben Whitaker was a starting linebacker on the football team heading into his senior year. For summer term he needed some extra credits and decided to take a community service-learning course where he could actually work hands-on in the community. He much preferred this kind of course for the summer because it gave him an opportunity to learn differently from the traditional classroom setting. Besides, he believed in doing community service, had been able to do it in high school, and was eager to continue doing so in college.*

*Ben's placement involved working at an outreach site for HIV-AIDS counseling. Ben had to participate in a full weekend of training before working at the agency, learning about HIV-AIDS and other sexually transmitted diseases, and also about preventive measures. Ben had some misgivings about the agency because he didn't really believe it was a good idea to offer counseling about sexual activity or to distribute condoms. He wasn't sure whether it encouraged people to go out and have sex or be more careful. He was also concerned because he knew he would be easily recognized as a football player and wasn't sure he would feel comfortable being identified while telling people how to have safe sex.*

Twice a week, for an entire afternoon, he would go out with the agency van that would stop in different high-risk neighborhoods, and he would talk to whomever came up to the van seeking help. The van also had HIV-AIDS test kits and distributed free condoms and information packets to those interested.

Ben was a little nervous at first about the neighborhoods that the van went into, wondering how safe they were, and whether anyone would actually approach the beat-up van. However, he soon saw first-hand how many people, men and women alike and of all ages, would come up to the van, ask for condoms, and talk about concerns about sexually transmitted diseases and related neighborhood gossip with the agency counselor. On occasion, people would also come into the van for a private HIV-AIDS test. As he observed the friendly and helpful interactions between the community members and the agency staff, he realized his safety fears had been unwarranted.

Slowly, over the course of the term, Ben began to become a believer in the agency's purpose and the van's work. He also got to know the counselor, an off-beat woman who in her own way was absolutely brilliant in reaching out to the community members, gaining their trust, and helping them to begin to take seriously the need for safe, protected sex. Ben marveled at how people in the neighborhood depended on her in so many ways to help them pull together their own sexual, personal, and professional lives—and get free condoms.

As Ben learned more about the agency's work, he also began to take seriously the importance of safe sex. He read materials from the agency and also went to the library and started to do outside readings on the topic. He began to become more and more knowledgeable.

As Ben was feeling more and more confident about all that he was learning, he started to think about the practice of his teammates and other friends with regard to sexual activity. Sure, there had been a talk about being careful not to get into sexual trouble and not to catch any diseases. But that had been the extent of it. Ben knew that from weekend to weekend some of his teammates regularly partied, had sex with changing partners, and, rarely if ever, used condoms or employed other safe sex practices. How did Ben know this? Well, prior to this class, he had been right there with those teammates doing all the things that he now realized could get him into a lot of trouble in terms of sexually transmitted diseases.

Ben also began to think much more about the entire business of sleeping around with multiple partners, the nature of relationships, his role as a male, and his position as a role model to many as a football player. Wasn't a lot of this essentially just about respect—respect for yourself, respect for women, respect for relationships, and respect for you and your partner's bodies?

Just like any good linebacker, Ben was on a mission, but this time it was not on the football field or about making a crushing tackle. Ben started talking openly with his friends about his community-service experience, and he decided to ask the medical team to set up some regular informational meetings available to all athletes. Yes, he was going to do his share to make sure student athletes learned about safe, protected sex, about the importance of using condoms, and the need to avoid getting—or spreading—sexually transmitted diseases. And, as was Ben's way, he was going to make certain that his own teammates showed up, paid attention, listened closely, and followed his lead.

## 5. Take Democracy Seriously: Participate Actively in Civic Life ◢◣◤

Those of us who have grown up in a democratic society often assume that our way of government will go on forever and ever. But a growing chorus of scholars warns that democracies are actually fairly fragile enterprises that may not endure unless they are cared for and looked after. That's our job, and that's your job.

Some things you can do to make your democracy stronger and enhance your college experience are listed, as are the reasons why these activities are so important. Remember, the United States is democracy of the people, by the people, for the people—and you are the people!

❶ Vote! When only a few people vote, it means that a small number of people are getting to make the decisions for the rest of us about who runs our cities, our states, and our country. That's not very democratic.

❷ Get involved, and participate in civic life in your community. An engaged citizenry makes for a strong democracy. As a student athlete, you also need to closely monitor and protect your study and practice time before devoting too much of your time to your civic responsibilities during college.

❸ Do community service. Make the concerns of your neighborhood and surrounding towns and cities your business. Yes, it does take all of us to keep the nation's democracy healthy and vibrant for future generations. If we don't care about the people in our community, state, or nation, we can't expect that our elected officials will care about us or our neighbors. Citizens in a democratic nation look after other citizens and take responsibility for the good of the whole.

④ Get a good education, and finish your degree. Democracies need educated citizens and leaders who can think critically, reason analytically, and size up complex problems from many different perspectives. An uneducated, uninformed citizenry is more likely to follow demagogues and fail to challenge bad ideas from wrongheaded leaders. College students like you, who will be well educated and involved in society, are our nation's best hope for a strong, diverse democracy.

## 6. Participate in Intergroup Dialogue

Imagine white students in a small class talking with students of color, gay students in conversation with straight students, men and women talking honestly, students meeting with their peers from different religious backgrounds, and U.S.-born students engaged in activities with international students. Across the country, more and more universities are establishing programs to help students engage in in-depth, serious conversations with fellow students from different social backgrounds.

It's hard for many students to find a safe space to ask one another the really hard questions about race, gender, sexual orientation, religious difference, and about life in general. If you're like the great majority of entering college students, it's highly unlikely that you've had the experience of a deep and sustained conversation with others about the important and enduring issues of differences, commonalities, equalities, and inequalities based on our social identities.

Most students, like you, are very eager for these conversations, yet we all know how hard it is to speak openly about our society's longstanding divisions and conflicts. Intergroup dialogues on college campuses—organized through courses, workshops, or retreats—are structured to give you and other students a chance to meet one another as individuals and as members of various social identity groups, develop a degree of trust in the dialogue group, and build a safe space in which to engage the truly difficult issues that so often divide us.

Students talk about intergroup dialogues as being transformative experiences. What is so exciting about them is that they give you a chance to open the doors to the potential of a diverse society and the dream of American democracy. It's a chance to participate in grassroots democracy, an updated, diverse version of the 19-century New England town hall meeting, where citizens took active control and responsibility for the life of the community and the democratic society. Instead of being held back by the fear and invisible walls that keep people apart, students who participate in dialogues are able to personally engage with their peers on campus and embrace a world that brings all people together.

Another advantage of intergroup dialogue is that, as research findings demonstrate, if you as a student engage with people from different backgrounds, you will learn and understand in deeper and more complex ways than your peers who remain safely in their own comfort zones. Finally, you are more likely to find that the professional world that awaits you as a graduating senior will be looking for someone just like you, a person who can work effectively with people from all different backgrounds as employees, co-workers, and supervisors.

This is especially important for student athletes. While your team may have a diverse mix of athletes, you spend most of your waking hours with this same small group of people. Don't miss an opportunity to participate in intergroup dialogues—it's a chance for you to gain the full benefit of an undergraduate education and to become an active participant and leader in our democratic society.

## 7. Collaborate with Your Peers

To succeed in your personal and professional life, you will need to have good collaboration skills so that you can work effectively with people you like and befriend, those you don't know well or don't like, those who come from similar or different backgrounds from yours, and even those who hold different or competing values and personal styles than you. As a college athlete, you've had enough team experience to understand the benefits and the potential difficulty of these group dynamics.

Colleges increasingly require students to work on group projects, participate in study groups, and write papers together. The research on study groups clearly demonstrates that students, both those more and less advanced, learn more in groups than by exclusively studying alone.

If you're like many other students, you may be thinking that study groups and group projects don't always feel like they're very worthwhile. They can take more time, are often complicated to schedule due to athletic commitments, require more social involvement, more effort, and can result in occasional struggles with one individual who does not come ready to do an equal share of the work. All of this reflects real life in the workplace and community, and these are important though sometimes unpleasant and painful skills to learn.

How do you make these collaborative projects work well and efficiently? First, you have to come prepared. Second, you have to come with a readiness to learn and cooperate. Third, you must be prepared to be open to working and learning in a manner of equality with people who may have different learning and working styles, who may have different goals and ambitions, and who come from backgrounds different from yours.

One of the common problems in work projects is that people often reinforce societal stereotypes in their collaborations. In math study groups, for example, men sometimes have lower expectations for the ability of women in the group and seek to dominate the discussion. Or Asian students are asked to do the statistical work. Be sure to check your own stereotypes and assumptions at the door and challenge others to do the same, especially if you get a vibe about being an athlete. Come with openness and high expectations for all participants.

It is important to determine how to share work responsibilities right from the start. If you're doing a group research project and paper, decide early on who will do which parts of the research—literature review, research and data collection, interviews, and so on—and who will take responsibility for the writing. You may decide that each person will write a section of the paper, but then someone will need to rewrite so the paper has one voice. Another option is for a person who does less of the data collection to take responsibility for writing a draft of the paper and then have others revise and rewrite. It's always important to set strict timelines and check-in dates to be sure that all the required work is getting completed with high standards.

Study groups work the same way. Schedule meetings early and frequently. You will not be the only student with additional commitments so the group has to work creatively to find times that work for everybody. Perhaps it makes it easier for the group to meet where your study table sessions meet. Practice schedules are usually manageable to schedule around, but if your travel or competition schedule makes it difficult for the group to meet, see if your instructor can provide assistance or suggestions.

Decide who will facilitate each study group and who is responsible for presenting which aspects of the study preparation. Sometimes everyone will need to be responsible for everything; other times you will want to share responsibilities. Decide on the ground rules for continued participation and under what conditions a person may be asked to leave the group.

Collaboration skills come into play in almost everything you do. Developing these skills will serve you well in your personal and professional relationships, your learning, your growth and love of life, and your professional and career development.

## 8. Model a Sustainable Lifestyle

How are we going to survive as a planet? And what steps are you going to take in your life to insure that we survive? As much as the college years are a time to take control of your identity, your studies, and your relationships, it is also a time to take responsibility for your imprint on the planet. The frightening dangers to our very survival as a species are well documented, and they will most certainly impact your lives and the lives of your children and grandchildren. You can no longer see yourself as just a consumer of the world's resources, but you also must reimagine yourself as a caretaker of the planet and begin to model your values.

While the scope of the climate and environmental crisis is daunting, it still calls for change in small steps by each individual as well as national and global policy changes. So, start to think about what small steps you can take in your life at college to begin to have an impact. First, find out the size of your carbon footprint, and make a list of the ways that you can reduce that footprint. Look at your daily practice using lights, electricity, technology, cars, gas, and air conditioning, and reevaluate your usage. What are your recycling habits? What are your consumption habits? What can you do to influence the products used by your athletic department for laundry, food, or recycling?

Do you know where your food comes from? Do your food purchases support sustainable agriculture? What is the history of the salmon you are eating—is it wild salmon or farmed salmon? What were the conditions of the farm and the cow and the workers and the meatpackers that led to the hamburger you are eating? How much corn and corn byproducts are in the everyday foods you eat, why is that the case, and what does it mean for the health of the ecosystem and for your health? And how do the agribusiness processes and the policy decisions about how much meat and corn that is produced affect global climate? What is the likelihood of you and people around the world getting e-coli or other diseases from eating dinner tonight?

What are the local initiatives in your college and town to transition toward a more sustainable planet? Do you or the college cafeteria make decisions to purchase locally grown food? Is there public transportation to get around town? Do you walk or ride a bike? How do we manage the impact on our planet of the increasing globalization of our communities? As study abroad becomes more of an expectation for your college studies, are there other options to create international experiences, learning, and social networks apart from increasing the amount of air travel and the resulting increase in jet fuel consumption? What policy initiatives can your campus, athletic department, and college town undertake to create a more sustainable present and future for all of us?

You might be tempted to think that these are matters to take up later, after you have finished your college education. But now, while you are in college, is exactly the time to learn about these issues and how they affect you, your career, your family, and your community.

# CHAPTER 7

# Health, Safety, Family, and Finances: It's All about the Team

## 1. Nurture Your Soul

As much as your mind and your physical body need your care, attention, and stimulation, so does your inner soul. Feed and nurture it and you will be that much stronger and more grounded to face each day. Beyond any material goals or even academic achievements, what is important to you in life? What are your values? When you get down to the essentials in your life, what matters most? What keeps you going each day? What is your purpose in life?

You will know if you are having academic troubles in your classes because your professor will speak to you or you will find yourself getting grades that are below your expectations. Your mind will let you know whether you are stimulated by your teachers and by the related intellectual content of the courses. Your body will tell you if you are not feeling well or if you have sustained an injury. It's just as important to have some mechanisms to keep track of whether your soul is healthy or aching.

Do people speak well of you, the person, not just of your athletic or other accomplishments or the clothes you wear? Do your friends like you because of your generous spirit, or do they like you because you own a car or have a new TV in your room? Do you like yourself because of your good looks, because of awards you have received, or because you like what you stand for in the world?

Do you feel good about who you are? Do you not only like the personality you present to others but also like the person inside whom you know better than anyone else? Can you not only live with yourself but also appreciate and respect who you are?

You may want to determine what things nurture your soul. It might be a good friendship. It might be good family relationships. You could be heartened by the story of someone's life that you read about in a book or saw in a movie. Perhaps you feel good after doing something good for another person, for your community, or for an animal or for the environment. You might need to learn something new and inspiring, appreciate a work of art or music, or gain insight into something you never understood before. Your soul might be nurtured by your connection with your faith or god or by appreciating the bounty of the earth when you eat some fresh fruit and vegetables. You might get this feeling from a deeply moving conversation with a friend or teammate, a teacher, your coach, a parent, or grandparent or from the joy of holding a newborn baby.

Being healthy has many dimensions. You know you need to take care of your body and mind, but be just as concerned with your soul. It is the essence of who you are.

## 2. Go to Sleep If You're Tired

"Don't get mono." That straightforward piece of advice comes directly from students. Many students get so busy with their lives that they push and push their bodies to the limit and beyond. Then, when they get sick, they are surprised that they had forgotten that important advice, which is actually about much more than just mono.

The advice is about looking after the health of your body. Feed it and sleep it and it will be there for you to fully enjoy all those wonderful, electrifying moments of college life. It will sustain you through some of the more difficult and stressful times as well. Ignore your body, and even if you don't get mono, you'll still have colds, be sluggish, and won't be able to participate at 100 percent—athletically, socially, or academically.

Don't forget to sleep. Pretty simple advice, right? The truth is that too many students get too little sleep on a regular basis and more than a few skip sleeping entirely. It's a myth that students don't go to bed in college before two in the morning or that no one starts studying till after eleven at night. A few students do study well after things quiet down in the wee hours of the night, but most students' academic productivity and retention decrease dramatically once they get tired. This is not rocket science.

Though eating and sleeping are things you've done your entire life, in a funny way, they are new experiences at college. Cafeteria food presents great opportunities, such as plentiful food and no need for cooking or washing dishes. It also presents new challenges that may lead you to eat more than you ever wanted or less than you really need. You should just follow the sound dietary advice given to everyone, whether or not they are in college, that you should do your best to eat healthy foods and exercise regularly. Yes, you may gain a few pounds or lose a few pounds due to all the changes when you first start college, including a new athletic routine. But if you're working out, and generally making healthy choices from the array of foods in the cafeteria or training table, you'll do just fine.

What you should concern yourself with is keeping a positive attitude and a good sense of self-esteem. It's much easier to do so when your body is getting nourished. Athletes don't usually forget to eat, but eating well all the time requires a conscious effort. This is especially true given your hectic schedule. Some students get so involved at exam time or during their involvement in some major campus activity that they skip meals, thinking they can get by until the next mealtime comes along. If you miss meals, you'll feel weaker, be more stressed, have less internal stamina to constructively manage all the activities in your life, and be more vulnerable to getting sick.

Don't forget to dress appropriately for the weather. If it's raining, don't worry first about fashion. Bring an umbrella or wear a raincoat.

You don't want to be walking around campus soaked all day. If it's cold and snowing, don't go out in a t-shirt and shorts. Wear heavy socks, a sweater or sweatshirt (hoodies work great), and maybe thermal underwear. Don't forget the importance of outerwear; wear gloves, a scarf, hat, a warm coat, and water-resistant boots with good traction. You don't want to risk an injury from falling on the ice. It's more fashionable to be healthy and participating in everything than lying in bed with a fever.

What about when you're starting to feel a little under the weather? Again, listen to your body. If your throat is sore, drink a steady stream of hot or cold liquids without caffeine. It's been scientifically proven that chicken soup really does work! If you're cold and it's snowing outside, dress warmly. If you're more tired than usual, get extra sleep. Talk to your athletic trainer to get additional advice and decide whether you need to see a doctor.

You're in college—you're smart, and you know all this advice. Practice it, and your body will thank you by working at full efficiency.

## 3. Visit the Counseling Center and Listen to Your Trainers and Health Professionals

Your college and the athletic department have invaluable resources available to support your well-being so that you can focus on your academic studies. Take full advantage of these resources and services. You are entitled to them. You shouldn't hesitate for even a second.

As an athlete, you will have medical treatment available to you through your athletic training facility, in addition to the other campus resources. Make sure you find out the procedures your trainers want you to follow if you need medical attention after business hours. Also, find out the procedures you are supposed to follow for more personal matters.

You may to go to the campus health center for sexually related issues, such as birth control or tests for sexually transmitted diseases (STDs). You may experience new problems at college or come with previously diagnosed problems and need continuing treatment for issues like headaches, eating disorders, vision problems, or depression.

You may experience difficulty with a previously diagnosed learning disability or may discover in college that you have a learning disability. The difference in the type and amount of academic work between high school and college often challenges the compensating strategies that worked in high school. It is not uncommon for students who did not need accommodations for learning disabilities in high school to need them in college. If you have a diagnosed learning disability or if you think you need to be tested for one, definitely discuss this with your academic and athletic advisors. Also, be sure to clear any prescription medication with the athletic department medical staff. Some prescription drugs could be considered banned substances and jeopardize your eligibility and scholarship.

Some colleges have a counseling center that is separate from the health center, but they are often closely integrated. Counseling centers schedule regular appointments but also almost always have walk-in hours when you can just drop in without an appointment and someone will be available to see you. Just like the health center, there is usually no cost or just a minimal payment to see a counselor. Several decades ago there was a stigma attached to seeing a counselor or therapist, but today quite the opposite is true Your athletic department will have a mental health professional (licensed psychologist, counselor, or social worker) on staff or easily accessible to you as well.

There are any number of reasons you may want or need to meet with a mental health professional while you're in college: You might be very homesick or might have a close relative at home who is not well, and you want to talk to someone about the situation. In the first weeks, you might find that you are having trouble adjusting to being on your own and going to college. Unsatisfactory athletic performance might be the cause or the effect of other problems you are experiencing. Or, your parents might call to tell you that they are divorcing or that there are financial difficulties because one parent has been laid off from work. You might find yourself in a relationship for the first time and need someone to talk to about it. You might be in a relationship that is breaking up, or you might be in a relationship with a person who is manipulative and abusive.

Athletic medicine departments and campus counseling and health centers are prepared to deal with weight issues, nutritional eating requirements, and eating disorders. If a student is sexually assaulted while on campus, the counseling center and health center are there to help. Athletes abusing drugs or alcohol may receive coordinated treatment from the campus counseling and health centers or community resources. Since substance abuse is a violation of athletic status, treatment is usually not available through athletic medicine departments.

In very extreme cases where an athlete may be suicidal, emergency measures established by your college campus should be followed. Academic difficulties can also be a cause of or result from other types of problems. Sometimes, when students have academic problems, the cause lies with issues that are not related to the classroom but that need to be addressed in counseling. Some students have problems managing their money, and they need to talk with someone about how to get financial issues, like credit card abuse, under control.

Even though athletes are able to receive most medical services through the athletic department, it's important for you to know about the campus mental health and medical resources in case of an emergency.

These services are part of your college's resources. They are for you, not just for others. Your tuition pays for these services, and you should take full advantage of them. If you're in doubt about whether your problem is serious enough to get help, by all means err on the side of going for help. Getting the treatment and support for your physical and emotional/mental health is part of growing up and becoming an adult.

## 4. Be Safe in Sex

Whether you're a man or a woman, straight or gay, you need to become educated about safe sex. If you don't know how to protect yourself and your prospective partner before you come to college, take the first days of college to get a crash course on the subject. You and your prospective partner's health and life depend on it.

As an adult, you will make your own decisions about whether or not, when and with whom to have sexual relations during your college years. The fact is, however, that large numbers of college students are sexually active and do engage in intercourse, and those who do, as well as their friends, need to know what to do to avoid unwanted pregnancy and sexually transmitted diseases.

Sexual choices are serious ones, with personal, emotional, social, and religious ramifications. Too many students are too skittish to talk about sexual relations and sex education, even though they've been exposed to TV shows, music videos, talk shows, and movies that seem totally consumed with sex. The consequences of unprotected sex can leave you with enduring and dangerous illnesses such as HIV-AIDS, unwanted pregnancies, and difficult personal choices about abortion or raising a child.

One of the best ways that sexually active people can avoid having unsafe sex is to remain sober. All kinds of bad judgments and ill-considered actions take place under the influence of alcohol. The likelihood of having unwanted and unprotected sex rises exponentially if you are under the influence of alcohol or other drugs.

There are some places and times on campus when one should be particularly on guard for the mix of alcohol and (unprotected) sex. For example, the first days of college, before classes start, are unfortunately notorious for parties with heavy drinking and with some upperclass students taking advantage of first-year students. Pre-game and post-game football parties are another time to stay sober if you don't want to get into sexual trouble. Finally, despite annual pledges of restraint in alcohol use, some fraternities and sororities continue to be places featuring out-of-control drinking and unwanted and unprotected sex. Beware!

Another way that sexually active people can avoid unprotected sex is to talk with their steady partners about safe sex. Be sure that both of you are committed to using protection and being safe every time you engage in sexual activity.

In a relationship, you and your partner should know how you might feel about an unplanned pregnancy. You may come from different backgrounds and cultures in which having a child at this stage of your life is perceived very differently. In the case of casual sex, it is even more important to protect yourself for these same reasons, in addition to the various sexually transmitted diseases associated with sexual intercourse. If you are not sure what to do to best protect yourself, talk to a medical professional. If it is uncomfortable for you to talk with someone affiliated with your athletic medicine department, go to the campus clinic. In addition to negatively affecting your academic and athletic dreams, the consequences of unprotected sex, in this day and age, can be life threatening.

Get educated and be protected. Get condoms and other protection for safe sex. Think about these issues now, well before you find yourself in a situation when it will be that much harder to start the discussion. Care enough about yourself and your friends to support one another to always be protected and prepared. This is everyone's responsibility: yours, your partner's, and your friends—men and women alike.

## 5. Make Smart, Informed, and Lawful Choices about Your Use of Alcohol and Other Substances

You're on your own at college. With regard to alcohol and drug use, most students have to do serious soul searching to figure out what choices they want to make about alcohol and drugs while in college. As a student athlete, however, you are in an entirely different circumstance. True, your parents won't be around to police your illegal underage drinking or your use of illegal recreational drugs. But you have to abide by the regulations imposed on you as a student athlete by the athletic governing bodies, your school, your coach, and the law. And the stakes are very high. You could easily lose everything you've worked so hard for, including your athletic status and scholarship.

The question of how you want to behave in college with regard to alcohol and other drugs is not one you can avoid. Alcohol and drugs will be widely available, and there will be both friendly encouragement and sometimes pressure from friends and social organizations to drink or use drugs, even from other athletes. Students you know and like will be inviting you into their rooms to drink, smoke marijuana, or try other drugs. Many off-campus parties will have alcohol, marijuana, and other drugs readily available. Athletes are far more likely to use and abuse alcohol than drugs. But you put yourself at risk as an athlete, especially if you are a highly visible or well-known athlete on your campus.

Before you come to college, think about how you want to handle these situations. It will be much easier for you to make sound decisions and exercise the required discipline of saying no if you're not caught off guard.

Think about why you want to drink. If it's because you can't feel relaxed or sociable without a few drinks in you, you should consider working on those issues without the crutch of a drink. Or perhaps you feel justified because you want to either celebrate or drown your misery during your season, or you want to hide the stress or anxiety you may be feeling about any number of things. You might feel justified but still may be violating rules and laws intended to prevent athlete use and abuse of alcohol and/or drugs. Using fake I.D.s or possessing or selling illegal substances raise additional serious problems and consequences.

Data on binge drinking on college campuses are now collected each year with little variation in the high rates of bingeing. Every year, news reports tell of college students taken to the hospital as a result of alcohol poisoning. Despite the clever and entertaining TV and print ads glamorizing alcohol use, most people know from personal experience that people who are drunk can be destructive, belligerent, and even violent. Add to that the aggressive nature of contact sports, and a drunk, aggressive athlete is a disaster waiting to happen. The deadly statistics of drinking and driving, as well as the dangers of alcohol and drug addiction, are all well known.

In addition to typical college choices about drugs and alcohol, elite athletes also have to grapple with issues related to illegal performance-enhancing drugs and substances. Your use of alcohol (and other drugs) in college is just one more decision you will need to make as a young adult. It will be *your* decision, not your parents', your coaches', your teachers', or your friends'. Most college athletes work very hard to achieve their peak performance by training and respecting their bodies. And, since college athletes can be subjected to required substance abuse testing, most athletes make sound decisions most of the time. It's ultimately a decision about your mental, emotional, and physical health.

Understanding why, whether, and how much you choose to use alcohol (or drugs) will help you discover more about the life you lead, about the degree of happiness and fulfillment in your life, and about the changes you might want to consider. These will be among the most important decisions you make in college. Choose wisely.

## 6. Know How to Avoid and Get Out of Dangerous Situations

The first rule of safety is that you should not put yourself in a situation that has a high potential to endanger you and others. If you don't do drugs, don't hang out with drug users or dealers. If you want to get home safely late at night, don't walk alone and don't go down dark streets. If you are sexually active but don't want to get sexually transmitted diseases, carefully protect yourself and have safe sex. If you don't want your room to be robbed, lock your door. If you don't want to cause a disastrous car accident, don't drink and drive.

The second rule of safety is to have an exit strategy if you should find yourself in a difficult or dangerous situation. Why do you need this second rule if you follow the first rule? The reason is that you can't always fully control your circumstances. Sometimes, through no fault of your own, you will find yourself in a dangerous situation. Athletes tend to be over-confident about safety risks because they think they are stronger than anybody who would try to harm them. But both men and women athletes have been injured in street crimes. Thus, the third rule is to always pay attention to your surroundings. Particularly in tough economic times, street crimes occur before dark or in places otherwise thought of as safe.

Imagine these situations:

- Picture yourself going to the library one night to study for an important exam. While you don't plan to stay there very long, you find you are doing good, focused work, and before you know it, it's two in the morning and the library is closing. You quickly gather your belongings and head home, this time, alone. You're tired and still thinking about the exam questions, and you just start walking across campus. As you walk along, you hear some people shouting things at you. You look back and see a couple of guys you don't recognize and who don't seem to be acting in a friendly manner. You look around some more and notice that you are the only student walking along this path. Fortunately, you have made a point of knowing where campus emergency phones are located. You know there are several phones on this path, so you hurry to the next one, stop at the phone, and make a quick 911 call. The campus police arrive in less than a minute.

- You go to an off-campus party with a friend. You hear that there will be great music and dancing, and your friend encourages you to come along. He has a car, so you ride with him to see his old high school buddies. At first the party is great fun. Before too long, however, everyone starts getting high. As an athlete, you're not particularly comfortable with everyone using drugs, but you try to enjoy the music. As it gets later, you realize that your friend is in no condition to drive safely back to campus. You offer to drive your friend's car, but he doesn't want to leave. Fortunately, you've planned ahead for this kind of situation. You have your cell phone and you carry extra money with you in case you ever need to take a taxi home. You call a taxi, and despite some uncomfortable waiting around, the taxi finally arrives and takes you back to campus.

- You've been getting closer to someone you are very attracted to. The relationship has been great in all respects and has not yet become a sexual relationship. One night you find yourself alone with this person in your residence hall room. Things move along fast—faster than you would have anticipated. You have made the choice to have sex, but realize that neither of you has a condom. Fortunately, you've thought about this ahead of time so you know what to do in this situation. Despite your desires and despite your concern that this might harm this new relationship, you firmly tell your partner that you won't have sex without protection. Your friend not only agrees with you, but expresses relief that you did not put either of you at risk of having unprotected intercourse. And, in the event that your partner has a different reaction and tries to talk you into "just this one time—nothing will happen," be prepared to say "no." You have too much at stake.

These kinds of scenarios or others like them may not happen frequently on campus, but they will happen. Try to recall situations you've been in where you wished you had used a good exit strategy and what it would have been. Also, imagine other possible scenarios in which you'll need a quick response to protect yourself. Be smart, not passive or frightened. It's just one more way to stay safe and healthy in college.

**Brianna Jones: "Who are my real friends?"**

*Brianna Jones was a big-time basketball star. People knew what she looked like, read about her in the paper, and debated her play on talk shows and in blogs. Even though she was one of several outstanding players on her team during her college career, she was nonetheless a woman in demand.*

*Everyone, it seemed, was her best friend. Old friends from high school and her home neighborhood, new students and staff on cam-*

pus, and other townspeople and alums all seemed to want to be her best friend. Facebook? It was simply astounding how many people "friended" her. She even had to use a different email account because she had pages and pages of friend requests.

Brianna was so overwhelmed by all the attention and pseudo-friendship that she began to shut down. Whom could she trust? Who sincerely cared about being her friend, and who just wanted to get close to her publicity, fame, and future fortune?

Brianna kept hearing how college was a place to make new friends. She wanted to expand her circle of friendships and not just hang out with other athletes. Brianna wanted to meet students in all majors, students who were interested in all kinds of college issues, but she also wanted to be careful and not get trapped by people who were just out to use her or who were taken in by her fame.

What Brianna was presenting to the world as "being open but careful," others perceived as arrogant and cocky. All of a sudden, her star of fame turned against her. Brianna's play and or her team's play continued to go well, but because she wanted a wide circle of real friends, not just athletes or insincere ones, word started to get out that Brianna was too impressed with herself to be friendly to others.

Then all of a sudden, or so it seemed, things started to go badly for Brianna. There was a family health problem, a friend from home was injured in a car accident, and she experienced conflicts with teammates. Brianna was under a lot of stress and it showed.

But what also happened in this time of despair was that her real friends stood out. While many of her "best" college buddies quickly moved onto the next great star athlete and left her alone to deal with her problems, Brianna's true friends stood by her when she needed them most. Her true friends, including some athletes as well as some non-athletes from class and her residence hall, were there for her when she wasn't in the public eye, when she wasn't scoring the winning basket, and when she was just feeling sad and alone.

Soon everything turned around, this time for the best: the family health problem was resolved, her friend was making a good recovery from the car accident, and Brianna and her teammates talked through their differences. The buzz about Brianna began to return, but she now had a better handle on how to present herself and handle the situation.

Brianna was again in the spotlight with all her previous positive stardom. The crowds of students and alumni again wanted to be her best friend. But Brianna had learned an important lesson about her public face and her personal friendships. As she was more confident in the strength of her truly close friends, she realized she didn't need to shut down entirely to her fans at her games or on Facebook. She began to feel more comfortable being friendly, showing appreciation for their interest, and flashing her big smile. She could now differentiate between fans and friends because she had learned anew that true friends will be there always, regardless of the circumstances, and that she could be open and trusting of sincere relationships.

It wasn't always clear or easy to tell who was being sincere and who not, but Brianna was learning quickly to make the distinctions. She loved her true friends; she grew very close to a small group of wonderful, caring people; and she was more than happy to give her hundreds or even thousands of so-called friends a "high five" and a smile as they passed by.

## 7. Keep in Touch with Family ⟶

You're enjoying your independence. You may miss home, but you are so happy to finally be at college and on your own. You want to show everyone you can do this. What are the rules about communicating with your family? Are you supposed to? Do you have to? Is it better to text, email, or call? How often? You're excited about the first days and weeks of college. There's so much going on, and you don't want to miss anything. How do the important people from back home fit in your new life at college?

If you are living on campus, make a point of staying there, especially in the first weeks of college. Some students who live relatively close to campus go home every weekend. That choice will rob you of the opportunity to fully invest emotionally in campus life, activities, and new friends. If you are at home too much, college doesn't really become home; you don't achieve the valuable growth and separation from your home and high school experience.

It's important to stay in touch with your family and other people close to you because they will be a part of your life forever. Your family members want to hear from you. Your parent(s) want to know if you're eating, staying healthy, and going to class. They will want to know how you're balancing school and athletics and how you like your new coach and your teammates. They are thinking about you, anxious about how you're adjusting, wondering how you're finding the demands of college, and whether you're making friends.

You have control over what you want to talk about with your family. You can ask for advice about classes, relationships, campus activities, and finances. Or you might decide that all you want to share with your parent(s) is that you're alive and well and doing okay.

In college, you are fast becoming an adult, just like your mother or father. You should be starting the work to adjust your relationship with your parents from that of child to adult to that of adult to adult. Certainly you will always be the child of your parent(s), but now it is time to start making the transition from being just the child to being the adult child, the adult friend, and the independent adult in relationship with your parent(s).

This good transition is not likely to happen overnight, but you should want your relationship to take some big steps forward over the course of your college education. It will happen when you shift from having your parents make decisions for you to asking them for advice so that you can make your own decisions.

You will see the change when you come home for school breaks or when you decide to spend your vacations with your friends and not your family. It will happen when you make an important and difficult decision even though you know that your parents would disagree with your choice.

For their part, your parent(s) and siblings may have their own adjustment issues with your being away at college. You are growing and changing in this relationship, but so, too, are your parent(s). They may have even more difficulty with this than you do. They will go through an adjustment period, just like you. If you're the first to go to college, it signals a period of substantial change in their lives, that their kids are growing up, as are they. If you're the sole child in the family or the last to go to college, then your parent(s) are in for an even greater adjustment, having to renew their adult lives and their married life as a couple, if they are married, or as a single individual living alone.

Stay in touch with your family. In the long run, you will most likely enjoy a deeper and more open relationship in the many decades that lie before you. While you're at it, ask them to send along a little care package. It's great to receive packages at college, whether they're large or small. It will give you a lift just when you need it, and it will make your parent(s) feel like they're needed and are still helping to raise you.

## 8. Adapt to Places Different from Home

You may have decided to attend a college away from home for the experience of being in a different place. This may include a different part of the state, the country, or even the world. You may have chosen a school in a place that has different weather, different food, and different people from your hometown. If you have, congratulations! You have put yourself in a situation where you can't help but grow and expand your horizons.

Students make decisions about where to attend schools based on a variety of factors. As student athletes, you have numerous additional athletic factors to consider. As part of your recruitment, you visited your school for the primary purpose of determining whether you and the school, including the athletic opportunity, are a good fit. During a recruiting visit, however, you may not have considered factors that will be more apparent to you once you are actually living in that location.

Is your campus in a big city, a small city, or out in the country? How does the campus and/or city look and feel compared to your hometown? How do students typically get around — walk, bus, bicycle, campus transportation, public transportation? Are there different seasons than you're used to? Will you see snow for the first time or experience twenty sunny days in a row for the first time? What is the major business or industry in the surrounding community, city, or state of your school? What is the demographic and socio-economic make-up of the student body? Are there certain well-known foods or traditions in this city or state? Do people sound different? Do they speak with an accent or use different words and expressions than you? Do people dress differently—more casually or more formally, more conservatively or more trendy than your hometown?

You will know the answers to some of these questions before you visit. You will find out more during your visit. And you will learn even more once you are actually living there and interacting with people on campus and in the city on a daily basis. Embrace the opportunity to be exposed to new and different people, places, and things. Do not be intimidated by the differences. Challenge yourself to appreciate the differences while you're living there. Remember, many of your fellow students will be in the same situation as you, coming from hometowns that are different from your campus community. Don't be surprised if by the time you graduate, you decide you like many of the features of your college town as much as the hometown you grew up in.

## 9. Know Your Money Matters

Money matters. You know money matters in business and government, but how much do you know about your own money matters and your personal financial situation? For many students, college is the first time in their lives they have to be aware of budgeting money, being responsible for paying bills, and managing credit and debit cards. This pertains to you whether you are on a full or partial athletic scholarship or are a walk-on receiving no athletic aid at all.

The financial aid office at your school should be able to answer all of your questions. There will be a liaison in the financial aid office who knows the ins and outs of working with athletes. It is important to fill out all of the financial aid forms, including the infamous FAFSA form, which is the key to all grants, loans, and funding options. Make sure you abide by all of the deadlines as offices outside the university often set and enforce deadlines so there are no extensions.

If you are lucky enough to be receiving an athletic scholarship, your athletic department will provide you with details about how and when the money from your scholarship gets applied to your university account. If you are not living in a residence hall, you are responsible for managing the process of getting your scholarship money into your checking account so you can pay your bills for food and housing. Pay attention to the fact that your scholarship will not cover all of your expenses. Find out ahead of time what you are responsible for paying.

It is often very misleading to get a large scholarship or financial aid check at the beginning of the term because it might seem like you have more than enough money for your expenses. This can lead to spending too much too soon and not having money for what you really need over the course of the time period it is supposed to cover. Unfortunately, too many college students get caught in this trap, which inevitably results in serious financial difficulty and consequences.

Other areas that often create unforeseen financial problems for typical college students include charges for cable TV, cell phones, and credit cards. When it comes to spending, remember that credit cards are not free money. They are not birthday gifts from a bank. They represent *your* money, and every dollar *you* spend, *you* will have to repay, often with high interest. Credit cards are a way of life today and when used properly are perfectly fine, but the problem is that college students are notorious for misusing credit cards.

The challenge facing you is to manage your credit and your credit card(s) carefully. First, you should ask the bank to set a low credit limit to help you from overspending, and you should only spend money on credit that you have set aside in your budget to spend. While banks may encourage you to overspend by offering low initial terms on interest rates, you need to know that that is how banks make money from credit cards. Those interest rate payments are what ruin people. You gain the advantage over the banks if you spend only an amount that you can pay off in full with every monthly bill.

Second, check your bill carefully before you sign for every purchase. Organize and store your receipts by month so you can review your monthly statement carefully. Make sure you are not charged for something you did not purchase and protect your identity.

If this is the first time you've had a credit card, you may be overwhelmed by the opportunity to go online or into a store, see something you want to buy, and buy it without paying cash. You also may forget today what you purchased on your credit last week and, as a result, your monthly bill may shock you. Avoid these traps! If you don't have the money to pay for an item in a store, don't buy it. If you see you are overspending, keep track of your purchases in a small notebook you keep with you during the day. College financial aid officers are also equipped to help students learn to budget and manage finances. Meet with a financial aid counselor if you need help managing your money.

Bank checks and debit cards would seem to be much simpler to use, but if you don't watch your checking balance, then you're likely to spend more than you have in the bank. The bank then will not honor your checks, and they will bounce. The bank will charge you high fees for going over your limit or bouncing checks, your credit will sink, and you'll be wasting a lot of unnecessary time on money matters instead of academic and social matters. You won't be happy.

Do not dip into your scholarship or financial aid to pay for credit card purchases. You will not be able to register for future semesters if you owe the university money. This could be the beginning of a very bad cycle. Don't ruin your college plans, and maybe even forfeit your eligibility, by getting sucked up into the credit card abyss that can ruin your finances and credit standing for years after college.

Student athletes *must* be knowledgeable about NCAA regulations regarding money. Student athletes should never accept money or free services, including food, for any athletic-related goods (like jerseys or signed footballs). You cannot exchange them for goods or services either. As an example of how even small amounts of gift money can be problematic, a former high-profile student athlete received a Christmas card in the mail with a very nice note and a $10.00 check intended as a Christmas gift. He was surprised and very touched that a stranger would take the time to do something so nice for him. Even though it was a sincere gesture and a small amount of money, he guessed he could not keep it. He took it to the Compliance Office, and he was right. The school returned the check with a polite thank you, explaining why the athlete could not keep it. The athlete wrote a nice thank-you note to the sender. This is a good example of how student athletes need to employ a "red flag" mentality and always remember that every aspect of any money transaction, large or small, is one critical way in which they are different from non-athlete students.

Learning to manage your money is one of the many ways you assume adult responsibilities in college. Just as in academics, the foundation of knowledge and experience you obtain early on enables you to be even more successful down the road. These are important skills you will build on and benefit from throughout your life.

## 10. Grow Up: Pick Up After Yourself and Do Your Own Laundry

How much responsibility did you have for keeping your clothes washed and your house clean before college? Many high school students enjoyed the luxury of somebody else worrying about laundry and cleaning, especially because extra-curricular activities usually don't leave time for much else besides homework. That will change in college. When you've gone through all your clean clothes and your laundry bag is full, it will be up to you to get them clean. When you throw socks on the floor they will not move until you pick them up.

Even if you can afford to pay a vendor to do your laundry and ironing in college, you should learn to do your own laundry. If you live close enough to home to take your laundry home to your mother or father, don't do this except in an emergency. These are good life lessons: It is important to know how to take care of your basic needs.

Now that you are not living in your family's home, you and your roommates are the kings or queens of your room, and you make the rules. If you don't clean up or if you wear dirty or smelly clothes, only you and your roommates have to live with the consequences. Of course, you may find there's more than a little peer pressure to stay on the clean and neat side of things. Your roommates, for instance, may have very different standards than you. They may strongly object to your clothes being strewn across the floor or hanging over the couch and desk chairs. Don't be surprised if they find it gross when you don't throw out your moldy cheese in the refrigerator, or you leave your cereal bowl, silverware, and glasses unwashed for days at a time. At the same time, your roommate might also object if you're the opposite extreme and expect the room to look like a magazine picture.

Your personal habits quickly become everyone's business on the floors of the residence hall and on your athletic team. Your peers will know more about your personal habits than you ever wished, and they'll talk about them. Peer pressure can be far more powerful than your father or mother asking you to clean up your room. Most important, however, is that you realize that you are responsible for taking care of yourself, and that you are mature enough to assume that responsibility. How you look, how your clothes appear, and how clean or dirty you keep your room is all about you. Your choices in these matters reflect on you and give people instant and long-lasting impressions about how you think about yourself. They will affect your relationships with roommates, friends, and teammates, as well as your own self-esteem and self-worth. It's yet another way you become an adult in college.

# Looking Beyond College: The Olympics of Life

## 1. Update Your Resume

Many high schools recognize the importance of resume writing so they help students write their first resume either by assigning it in a class or making it part of the college application process. If you did not have to write a resume in high school, you should make it a priority to write one soon. Why now, you might ask, since you are not applying for a job at the moment or have already been admitted to college? A resume is a useful tool to tell the world who you are, and you will need it for any number of reasons during college.

You may be asked to provide information about yourself for such things as internships, nominations for various types of awards, summer jobs, introductions in programs where you are speaking or participating, applications for leadership positions, and other similar opportunities. Some of the time you will be asked specifically for a resume while other times you will be asked to provide information that can be readily found in your updated resume.

If you did write a resume in high school as part of your college application, it is already out of date because you are in college now! Keep your resume updated whenever you have something to add, but at least at the end of every school year. That way, you will always have an up-to-date version ready to give when asked. As you apply for different types of jobs or internships, you may want to have different versions of your resume that highlight your qualifications for particular types of positions. You may also want to have a general version that can be used to provide information about you.

There are many different types of resumes and endless resources about how to write one. You can find good templates and sample resumes on the Internet, in books, and in your college career center. It is very helpful to look at samples of different types of resumes to get ideas and a better understanding about how different styles accomplish different goals. When you start to write, remember that one of the most basic resume-writing principles is to use action verbs for all of your descriptions. Be sure to work with the professionals at your school to come up with the best possible format and version.

At this stage of your life, since you have had only limited experience outside of attending school, use a resume format that allows you to emphasize your skills and competencies. Of course, you should also include any work experience you have, in addition to volunteer experience, awards, accomplishments, and acquired skills, including hobbies and recreational skills. Taken together, this information provides the reader with a picture of you as a complete person.

Resumes should be considered living documents; they grow with you. Each year of college will provide you with more accomplishments and experiences to add to your resume. The more frequently you update your resume throughout college, the easier it will be to produce the version of your resume when you need it most—when you are seeking a position as a college graduate.

## 2. Solicit Letters of Recommendation

Every job, internship, study abroad program, and graduate school will ask you to provide letters of recommendation and references. Once you're in college, it will no longer be good enough to get a letter from your favorite high school teacher or coach, somebody you worked for, your clergyperson, or a friend of the family who has seen you grow up and flourish.

Faculty members, graduate student instructors, advisors, and coaches at your college will be the most important source of letters of recommendation for you during your college years and beyond. You may find that you need these letters as early as the first semester of your first year of college. If you are looking for a summer internship, a research assistantship, admission to a specific academic program or major, or a scholarship or award, you will be asked to provide a letter from a faculty or staff member on your campus.

When you apply to graduate school or a professional school program or are applying for jobs, you will be required to submit letters from at least two or three faculty members (professors or graduate student instructors) who will write outstanding letters on your behalf. Assemble your recommendation portfolio throughout your college years. Most faculty members will be more than willing to write a letter for you, but only if you have developed a relationship with them or have caught their attention through your comments in class discussion, by writing an exceptional paper, or by visiting office hours. Your letters will be stronger if your positive attributes are fresh in the minds of your professors. A small number of very special faculty, usually those who have been so impressed with you that they are willing to serve as your champions, will go out of their way to initiate calls and contacts on your behalf. They will keep you in mind when they hear of scholarship opportunities, summer internships, special study programs, and research assistantships. They will make it their business to be sure you get into the best graduate programs.

Some people will be willing to write letters but will not be reliable about deadlines. You need to keep tabs on whether the letters you have requested have been submitted in a timely manner. Only ask people to write recommendations if you know they can write you a strong reference. If you can't depend on a faculty member to write a letter for you on time, you are better off finding a replacement.

When you do ask for a letter, you want to make the process as easy as possible. If you like this professor so much that you are asking for a reference letter, it's likely that many other students are as well, and your letter is just one of several that the professor is writing. Offer to meet to discuss the role this letter plays in your portfolio and what you would specifically like to be addressed in the letter. Explain what jobs, programs, or graduate schools you are applying to and provide an updated copy of your resume, any forms that need to be filled out (usually you will have to complete part of the forms), a short written reminder about the purpose of the letter, a personal statement (if part of the application), and the due date. If it's possible to send the letter via email or through a website, ask if electronic or snail mail is this professor's preferred method. If the latter, include a stamped, addressed envelope. Let your recommender know the eventual outcome of your applications—he or she will be interested to hear.

The key to asking for letters of recommendation is to know faculty or others well enough that you can approach them, and know with confidence that they will be able to provide a positive reference in a timely manner. Your first task in securing references is building your relationships. Faculty will be pleased and honored that you have asked and will be eager to learn that you have succeeded in your job search or in your pursuit of advanced graduate and professional degrees.

## 3. Figure Out the Best Ways to Use Your Summers

In high school, summer meant time for vacation and work, with physical conditioning and practice starting a few weeks before school. Your vacations were likely based on your family circumstances and commitments. Your job was based on what was available in your hometown, perhaps selling clothes at the mall, waiting tables at a diner, being a lifeguard at a local pool, or doing office work for a family friend. In college, your coach's expectations for summer will determine the choices you have for how to spend your summer. Find out early on what the expectation is for your team and your athletic scholarship commitment during the summer.

Be strategic about your summers. You need them to help you stay on top of your game, both academically and athletically, but that also means taking time to replenish yourself to take on another academic year. You don't want to start a new year burned out from the prior year. In addition, you may want to go home, spend time with your family, get off campus, and eat home cooking for a few days or longer.

You may be expected to stay on your college campus to work out and train under the watchful eyes of your team's professionals. You may want to take classes over the spring or summer because it makes sense in your degree plan, or because you need a scholarship check to help pay your expenses.

Sometimes, if you've had a very intense academic year, the best choice might seem to be to do as little as possible. Clear your head, get some sleep, and rest your body and your brain. That's a reasonable plan, at least for a week or two. After that, you'll find yourself extremely bored and increasingly annoying to your family and friends because you are used to being so busy. If you feel you need a few intensive weeks to "chill," make sure you have a plan for the rest of the summer.

Colleges offer all kinds of stimulating summer learning programs and many that you can elect for degree credit on campus or at home. Take the time to really explore your options before you make your summer plans. There are study abroad opportunities and research assistantships with faculty on campus or abroad. Some college departments have special field classes, such as literature and creative writing programs at camp-like sites off campus, or geological or oceanographic expeditions to interesting sites in the mountains or oceans. Many athletes want to learn or increase their coaching skills, and many schools offer course credit for experiential learning.

If you are not living in a residence hall, most students who stay on campus are able to find housing that is cheaper during the summer than the academic year. Depending on your scholarship and aid package, you may also be able to get a job and work for money. There may be jobs at local businesses, but there are also opportunities to work on campus in research labs, libraries, residence hall dining rooms, orientation programs, or giving campus tours or doing groundskeeping and facilities work.

If you are not required to stay on campus and you plan to return to your family home, you will have an edge in saving money for the next year since you're not paying rent for spring or summer. At home, you may be able to continue to work at jobs you held during high school or return as counselors to camps you attended when you were younger. You may be able to teach or coach your sport at a summer camp or community recreation program. Other students, particularly in professional schools, may find paid work related to their majors. Internships in your projected professional area are another great use of your summer time. More internships offer college credit than money these days so find out whether an internship is paid or volunteer before you apply. You will have to pay for the college credit so find out if your scholarship covers financial aid in spring or summer. Some colleges let you pay for summer internship credits with your fall tuition. Your school or athletic department may be able to help you find internships, but you should plan on doing the bulk of the research, informational interviewing, and applications on your own.

As always, given the potential for internship or job offers on the basis of your athletic status, be proactive about checking with your compliance department for guidelines before you accept an offer.

**Alex Martin: "Help! I'm drowning in my sport."**

*To the outsider, it appears very cool. All the varsity athletes get a wardrobe of athletic wear that's not even on the market. They stand out as special. They've made the team. They are the ones that everyone cheers for.*

*For Alex Martin, however, the special athletic apparel was suffocating. It marked him. It defined him. It was 24/7 athletics. He felt it said he was about athletics and nothing else.*

*Alex loved to play hockey. He loved the team and the competition. He loved his teammates and his coach. He couldn't possibly think of having had a better experience in college without playing hockey. True, he wasn't the best on the team, but he started every game, and he was a player, a force to be reckoned with on the ice.*

*But Alex also had other interests. Hockey was clearly not in his future, at least professionally. Besides, he wanted to pursue a career in* business. Business was another one of his loves. He wanted to expand his circle of friends and associations in college beyond athletics, and he wanted to be friends with others not solely based on his athletic talents and hockey playing. But that athletic clothing—he wore it everyday and, of course, it gave him away as the athlete.

In what some saw as a radical move, Alex woke up one day, put away the "special" gear, and wore some nice slacks with a shirt and a tie to class. To his teammates and athletic peers, this was shocking. Boy, did they razz him. Alex was one of the good guys, so no one was mean to him, but they sure enjoyed making fun of the man in the tie. And Alex wasn't too bad giving it right back to them, too.

Over time, the tie became Alex's persona. His new motto became "make new friends but keep the old," just like the children's song. Alex really did love his teammates and athletics. There was no way he was about to lose their friendship.

Still, Alex was comfortable with his identity. He knew who he was and who he wanted to be. Alex knew he was not going to be a professional athlete. What he desired was to become very successful in business, and he needed and wanted to become comfortable in the business community.

The tie stayed. The next summer Alex found a great internship with a local business. He made friends with students interning who attended other universities and with the younger adults in the local business community.

The fun and the jokes also stayed. But Alex's teammates respected him for the tie, despite the jokes. They saw that he was comfortable *with his own identity, that wearing a tie didn't mean sacrificing or compromising his athletic and team loyalties, and admired that he could bridge the two communities so well. They knew he was on the road to success after college and after hockey.*

## 4. Use the Power of Networking

Networking has become such a universally recognized and necessary skill that you have probably done it already, even if you didn't know you were doing it! The dictionary.com definition of networking is "a supportive system of sharing information and services among individuals and groups having a common interest." In practice, this means connecting with people you know, about things you are interested in (careers, jobs, or opportunities), and that you may have in common. The best case scenario in networking is that each person you network with is willing to connect you to other people who can provide additional information, contacts, and networking opportunities.

In high school, networking may have meant you seeking out people, or others seeking you out, who would be able to share insights and opinions about the various colleges you were considering. Social networking sites have become an accepted and integrated aspect of our professional and social culture. But, never underestimate the importance of face-to-face, in-person interaction. You can't feel the warmth of a handshake over the Internet.

As a college student athlete your uses for networking will include both academic and athletic opportunities. Many networking conversations also take the form of "informational interviews," or interviews with a person about a company, profession, or skill without a specific job on the line. There are four basic "always" rules for networking (and informational interviewing) that will help ensure you achieve the maximum potential outcome.

1. *Always* be on the lookout for networking opportunities. Anyone you know or meet may be able to provide you with useful information and additional contacts. You can't be shy about asking to meet with people. Have a standard line in mind that you use when asking to meet with people you know and with people you don't know. Ask for business cards and keep them organized with notes on the back about who that person is, how you met, and any other useful information. Print your own calling cards so you can exchange cards with people you meet. Keep more detailed notes well-organized and in a binder.

2. *Always* be prepared. Do your homework, and don't waste your networker's time. Make sure you have done whatever research you can on that person's job or profession so you know how that person might be able to help you and what questions to ask. Make a list of questions, and be prepared to take notes during the conversation. If you are meeting in person, suggest a coffee house or a place where you can afford to pick up the tab. As athletes, you have to be

careful about not allowing the networker to pay for you. It could be an extra benefit so check with your compliance office to be sure you know the rules about this. Dress appropriately, and remember that you only get to make one first impression.

❸ *Always* leave a networking conversation with names of other people to contact. Ask your networker to follow up with the prospective contacts via an email or phone call to let him or her know you will be making contact at his or her suggestion. Get the complete contact information of your current and prospective networkers, and be sure to follow up.

❹ *Always* send a thank-you note. Handwritten notes are best, post cards with pictures of places where you live are novel and are often appreciated, and email is often acceptable as well. If you want to stand out in that person's mind, do something other than email. Stay on that person's radar screen by sending a short email after you meet with contacts he or she suggested. Touch base every now and then just to keep the network alive.

Networking is an extremely effective and powerful tool. Chances are your athletic status will provide additional opportunities for networking. Follow these rules, and go for it!

# 5. Market Your Transferable Athletic Skills

The concept of utilizing transferable skills is not new in the academic or professional worlds. What it means is that you should recognize those skills you use in one context and identify how using those skills would look in another context. Often people do not realize they have skills and strengths that will carry over into other areas. For instance, when companies downsize and employees are laid off or their jobs become obsolete, career counselors help them understand what type of work they can do based on the skills they used in their prior positions.

This concept is also very useful for students entering the workforce, especially for student athletes who have less time than most other students for real work experience but whose experience as college student athletes provides important transferable skills to the work world. For example, student athletes are focused, committed, responsible, well organized, and efficient workers. In order to be successful, college athletes are also highly motivated, disciplined, and experienced in the need for precise training and preparation.

You have the benefit of developing excellent team skills and the opportunity to develop excellent leadership skills. You also know how to work individually and in smaller groups. You are used to realistic performance assessments and can accept constructive criticism and instruction about how to improve. You are used to authority and regimentation. You understand the concept of taking something forward from the idea stage to the execution and follow-up stages. You are used to striving for perfection, facing significant adversity, and being able to adapt to different and often unpredictable circumstances. You are able to think on your feet, make quick assessments and adjustments midstream, and you've learned to anticipate the behaviors of others.

Additionally, you understand the importance of community service, giving back, and mentoring those behind you. You are poised in the public eye, confident, self-assured, and strongly believe in your ability to succeed. You lead a healthy lifestyle; you eat right, exercise, and take good care of your body. Who wouldn't hire you? From an employer's point of view, you're a solid investment. These are the characteristics and skills that enabled you to be a successful college student athlete and that will make you a successful professional.

Be proud of including these transferable skills on your resume, cover letters, and interviews, along with your other experiences and skills where you have a demonstrated track record. Your mission is to learn how to market these skills outside of your sport. Learning how to talk about yourself in a way that addresses how these skills helped you succeed thus far, and how they will be the foundation of success in future endeavors, will make you an attractive and competitive applicant for an internship, job, or graduate school.

## 6. Ready, Set, Go: The Next Stage Is Your Career

College is the time to begin thinking seriously about career choices. As you explore the world of ideas, it's a time to find out about yourself—your likes and dislikes, your skills and challenges—and what kind of issues and tasks you find most stimulating. It's also a time to examine how you might fit best in the professional world of work.

It is not a good idea to think of your college education as career training. If you think of college as simply training for a profession, then you may get a good job credential from your college in the form of your diploma, but you will have missed out on a good college education. College is about learning and education. What you learn will no doubt be critical in whatever professional field you choose, but you should focus on learning as your priority.

Career exploration starts with taking a wide variety of courses to get an idea of where your interests lie. A course or experience that you don't like can be just as valuable as a positive experience in which you discover what you do like. Many students change their majors, and it is not uncommon to change from a narrowly focused major to a broader field of study or a major that affords you more flexibility in course selection and degree requirements. Explore, but be selective about what you take on in addition to your sport.

Find an internship or get a job in a field that carries some initial interest for you. As you get more serious and focused about your studies, go to the career center or your academic department to find out how your academic interests line up and prepare you for different kinds of careers. You'll be surprised at how expansive your opportunities are regardless of your major. Every professional position will require you to be able to think critically, broadly, and innovatively. You will be called on to do a wide range of tasks and to use a variety of skills in almost any field you choose. You may change careers more than once or twice, and you will certainly be required to retool and reconceptualize your work even in the unlikely event that you stay in the same career over a lifetime.

As you pursue a major, you will want to begin assessing the need and opportunity to attend graduate or professional schools. You also may decide to go directly into the workforce. Be sure to keep all of your options open. While you may feel today that you can't imagine attending school beyond your undergraduate degree, you may feel differently as you enter your senior year of college. Similarly, going directly into the workforce after college is by no means an indication that you won't ever decide to attend graduate school.

Students who enter college with clear pre-professional goals, like business, law, medicine, and especially engineering, will have a much more defined curriculum right from the start. While that training is important for your professional preparation, be careful to hold onto as much of the unique opportunity to take a wide array of courses. Take full advantage of your elective courses. Don't miss out on an undergraduate education because you are in such a hurry to advance professionally. You'll be working most of the rest of your adult life; your college education comes only once and for just a very few years in your lifetime.

A college education is essential for professional careers today. Take advantage of your education to begin thinking about and preparing for your professional life. At the same time, don't be so focused on what's ahead that you don't allow yourself to fully experience and enjoy today the gift that a college education represents.

# 7. Remember Your College Accomplishments

You will have numerous accomplishments—academic, athletic, service, and leadership—during your college years. Be sure to make a note of them in a journal or in a file. Even though you think you will always remember them without recording them, most likely you won't. If someone close to you offers to make you a scrapbook, accept the offer thankfully. From the moment you graduate high school, time will go by so quickly that unless you have an intentional, organized system for keeping memories, you will lose track of much that you'll want to remember.

Some of your accomplishments will be in the academic arena. You may get comments from a professor expressing what an outstanding essay or paper you've written. Keep that paper and hold onto those special words. You may be more formally recognized by being placed on the college honor roll or acknowledged at a college honors ceremony. You might be invited to serve on a university policy committee or to give input into departmental curricular projects. You may win a prize for poetry, creative writing, or artwork, or you may be invited to attend a conference to talk about your research.

Your athletic accomplishments will be a very special part of your college experience. Your wins and losses will only tell a very small part of the story. You will have endless stories to recount to your children, and even grandchildren, about your life as a college athlete, the wondrous accomplishments, and your teammates who have become lifelong friends.

Other accomplishments will be based on your personal and community achievements. You might have the joy of knowing you helped make somebody's life better or found a way to make yourself a better person. You may have surpassed a goal you had set for yourself before coming to college. You may win a scholarship for civic involvement, be elected or appointed to a leadership position in an organization, or get a promotion in your research lab.

Keep a record of these tributes, awards, honors, accomplishments, and stories. Someone you admire may say something very complimentary about you—write in a journal how you felt. If you're not the kind of person who keeps good files or notes, then make sure you make good mental images of your accomplishments, and maybe even a picture. Graciously accept the recognition you deserve and receive. You don't need to feel you're gloating to feel good about yourself. Try to hold onto the special moment when you received a compliment from someone you respect, a fun day with a good friend, or praise from one of your professors.

When you begin college, it will seem like you have an endless road ahead of you. Before you know it, you will be a sophomore. As a junior, all of a sudden you'll realize you're halfway through. Chances are, you'll wake up as a senior one day and want to slow down the process because you're about to graduate and leave this special time in your life. Cherish and hold onto your best memories, even as you continue to create special, new ones each and every day. Congratulations and good luck!